Redeemer in the Womb

JOHN SAWARD

Redeemer in
the Womb

Jesus Living in Mary

IGNATIUS PRESS   SAN FRANCISCO

No single translation has been followed for the Scripture references. On occasion I have made my own. The Psalms are cited according to the numeration in the Vulgate.

— J. S.

Cover art: Boucicaut: Hours
(Early fifteenth century)
"The Visitation", Musée Jacquemart-André, Paris
Bridgeman/Art Resource, New York

Cover design by Riz Boncan Marsella

© 1993 Ignatius Press
All rights reserved
ISBN 0-89870-427-8
Library of Congress catalogue number 92-74111
Printed in the United States of America

*To Anthony Cardinal Bevilacqua, Archbishop
of Philadelphia, with gratitude and respect.*

*And for our first grandchild and every other baby
who, as the Redeemer once was, is waiting to be born.*

CONTENTS

FOREWORD

It would be difficult for me, as a priest, to say over a piece of bread the words, "This is my body", over a cup of wine, "This is my blood", without feeling the presence of Mary. For me, the Sacrifice of the Mass is not only a spiritual and mysterious re-presentation of the crucifixion, death, and Resurrection of Jesus; it is similarly his conception in the womb of Mary and his Incarnation.

In the divine plan of salvation, Jesus was conceived and born of a woman. We have no way of truly knowing if it could have been otherwise, but since this is the way it was, it seems reasonable to ask if the Redeemer would have come at all had Mary refused the invitation to become his Mother.

What happened in Mary, of course, happened by the power of the Holy Spirit who "came" upon her. What happens in each Mass happens through the power of the Holy Spirit, the "coming" of the Holy Spirit upon the elements of bread and wine. Is Mary somehow present? Does the Holy Spirit continue to work through her? Could the crucifixion have taken place without the Incarnation, the Incarnation without the conception, any of these salvific acts except through Mary? The potential for theological reflection is fascinating. It is the kind of theological reflection that marks the provocative writing of John Saward in this book, *Redeemer in the Womb*.

It is a privilege for me periodically to conduct retreats on Mary, including special retreats for the Sisters of Life, a contemplative-apostolic community of women consecrated by vows of poverty, chastity, obedience, and the protection of human life. I speak always of the intimacy between Mary and the Redeemer in her womb, as reflected in the visitation to Elizabeth. We are told that it was when Elizabeth heard Mary's *greeting* that the baby in her own womb, John the Baptist, "leaped for joy" (Lk 1:41–44). Older theologians used to tell us that at that instant John the Baptist was purified of original sin. If so, could this be except by way of the presence of the unborn Jesus in Mary's womb, radiating his power into the womb of Elizabeth? Yet if the effect on John, whatever it was, came by way of the presence of Jesus, it was Mary's greeting—the word from her lips—that somehow seemed to Elizabeth to channel this effect on the infant in her own womb.

Such simple reflections on my part cannot begin to do justice to the thoughts revealed through Saward's text but are offered here simply to suggest the possibilities in exploring the nature of the relationship between Mary and the unborn infant Jesus. Unlike my own merely pious speculations, however, Saward combs the Scriptures, the Fathers of the Church, and later writers, even the icons of various periods, for thoughts hitherto unknown to many, almost certainly, *most* readers. My thoughts on the intimacy between Mary and her unborn child will be enlarged in future retreats because of Saward's insights.

This is a most unusual study and a contribution to Mariology of exceptional interest. Even more, it should prove to be an extraordinarily rich guide for meditation. I can see myself pondering it for years to come.

+ JOHN CARDINAL O'CONNOR
June 6, 1993
ODaU-M

ACKNOWLEDGEMENTS

This book was written in England, but finally prepared for publication in America. I have therefore transatlantic debts of thankfulness to repay. The original suggestion that I should draw out the 'pro-life' implications of Catholic faith in the Incarnation was made several years ago by Father Michael Kelly, parish priest of Shipley in Yorkshire. He knows already of my gratitude for that initial spur—I telephoned him the evening the manuscript was completed—but I am glad to take this opportunity to thank him in print. The research for the book was pursued while I was Professor of Dogmatic Theology at Ushaw College, Durham. I shall never lose my sense of privilege at being able to teach at the seminary that descends directly from the English College, Douai, and so includes among its alumni many of the martyrs of England and Wales. I thank my former colleagues and students for all I received from them during the last twelve years. Finally, I want to express the great pleasure I feel at joining the faculty of St Charles Borromeo Seminary, Philadelphia. To all those who have so warmly welcomed me into the 'City of Brotherly Love', especially Monsignor Daniel Murray and Monsignor Richard Malone, I say with all my heart, albeit in an unredeemably English accent, 'Thank You'.

— JOHN SAWARD

September 8, 1992   St Charles Borromeo
The Birthday of the   Seminary
Blessed Virgin Mary   Overbrook

INTRODUCTION
JESUS LIVING IN MARY

O Jesu vivens in Maria,
Veni et vive in famulo tuo,
In Spiritu sanctitatis tuae,
In plenitudine virtutis tuae,
In perfectione viarum tuarum,
In communione mysteriorum tuorum.
Dominare omni adversae potestati
In Spiritu tuo ad gloriam Patris. Amen.

God the Son became man at the moment of his conception by the Holy Spirit in the Blessed Virgin's womb.
Then, for nine months, he whom the heaven of heavens
cannot hold was housed, as a real human baby, within
his Mother's body.[1] 'A woman', said Chesterton, 'was
his walking home.'[2] The first stage of the divine Word's
human life was literally 'in Mary', in her womb. *O Jesu
vivens in Maria*. . . . Before he was among us, he was
inside her.[3] Most contemporary Christology, with some
noble exceptions, has little to say about what John Donne

[1] Prudentius says: 'The Virgin's ready faith drew Christ / Into her
womb and safely hid him there till birth' (*Apotheosis*, lines 583–84; PL
59, 970A).
[2] G. K. Chesterton, *The Queen of the Seven Swords* (London, 1926),
37.
[3] Exactly where, asks St Augustine, did the Son of God empty himself and take the form of a servant? 'In the Virgin Mary', he replies.
(*Sermo CXCVI* [*In Natali Domini XIII*], 1; PL 38, 1019).

I

called this 'well-beloved imprisonment'.[4] In fact, the historical mysteries of the life of Jesus as a whole do not
nowadays receive the attention given them by the theologians of the past—for example, by St Thomas Aquinas
in the third part of his *Summa Theologiae*, where twenty-
six questions on the hypostatic union and the attributes
of Christ's humanity are followed by thirty-two on the
course of his human actions and experiences from virginal conception to Ascension.[5]

This is an essay in reclamation. First, with the aid of the
Church's Fathers and chief Doctors, drawing on Christian philosophy, liturgy, poetry, and iconography, it seeks
to recover and reconsider a forgotten pearl from the treasury of revelation—the nine months of Jesus' embryonic
and fetal life in Mary. Secondly, since the God-Man reveals not only God to man but man to man,[6] I am inviting
my readers to look again, this time in the light of Christ,
at the womb-weeks of their own and every human life.
I am going to suggest that we re-read this first chapter
of the human story and find afresh its beauty, truth, and
goodness. It is only our estranged faces that have missed
this many-splendoured thing.

---

[4] 'Holy Sonnets', *The Poems of John Donne*, ed. Herbert J. C. Grier-
son, 1 (Oxford, 1912), 319.

[5] Among present-day theologians attempting to re-awaken interest
in the mysteries of the life of Jesus, we should mention Hans Urs von
Balthasar, Louis Bouyer, and Leo Scheffczyk. The last of these has edited
a valuable collection of essays on the subject: *Die Mysterien des Lebens
Jesu und die christliche Existenz* (Aschaffenburg, 1984).

[6] *Gaudium et spes* 22; *Decreta*, 709f.

I

THE MOMENT GOD BECAME MAN

In the Church of the Annunciation in Nazareth there is a plaque with this inscription: *Verbum caro hic factum est* —'the Word was made flesh *here*'. It was *there*, in that particular place, 'a city of Galilee' (Lk 1:26), that God became man. But we can be even more specific: it was in the womb of a virgin named Mary (cf. v. 27) that God the Son, without ceasing to be true God, assumed a complete human nature into the unity of his divine person and became true man. Moreover, according to the Church's teaching, we can be precise about the moment of the Incarnation: it took place when the Virgin Mary said to the angel, 'Be it done unto me according to thy word' (v. 38). It was exactly then that, by the overshadowing of the Spirit, a body was fashioned from the Virgin's flesh and blood, a rational soul created and infused into the body and, in the same instant, the complete human nature united to the divine Word. There were no successive stages in this taking of manhood; the body did not come into being before the soul, nor the soul before the body, nor were either ever other than his, God the Son's: the flesh was conceived, ensouled, and assumed simultaneously.

The coincidence of the virginal conception and the hypostatic union is a defined doctrine of the Catholic faith. In the words of the 'Formula of Union' agreed between St Cyril of Alexandria and the Antiochene bishops in 433 and canonized by the General Council of Chalcedon in 451, 'we confess the holy Virgin to be Mother of God, because God the Word was made flesh and became man and from the very moment of conception united to himself the temple he had taken from her.'[1] Origen's theory that the soul of Christ pre-existed the creation of his body was condemned by the provincial Council of Constantinople in 543, as was the opinion that the body was first formed and only later united to the soul and the Word.[2] This judgement was later confirmed by Pope Vigilius (d. 555). In 675 the eleventh provincial Council of Toledo declared that it was in his 'wonderful conception' that the Word was made flesh, and five years later the Third General Council of Constantinople officially approved the synodal epistle of St Sophronius of Jerusalem (c. 560–638), which contains this relevant passage:

> He truly became man who is ever acknowledged to be God, and is shown to be in his Mother's womb who is in the bosom of the eternal Father, and the timeless accepts a beginning in time. He did not become these things in unreal appearance (as the Manichees and Valentinians think), but in truth and reality he emptied the whole of himself by the will that is his own and the Father's, and assumed the whole mass [of our nature], flesh consubstantial with us, a rational soul of the same kind as ours, a mind like ours. For man is and is known to be all these things; and

[1] DS 272. On the different opinions of the Fathers about the timing of Christ's conception (before or after Mary's *fiat*), see M. Kellison (of the English College, Douai), *Commentarii ac Disputationes in Tertiam Partem Summae Theologicae S. Thomae Aquinatis* (Douai, 1633), 309f.

[2] DS 404–5.

he was made man in truth at the very instant of his conception in the all-holy Virgin.[3]

More recently, Pope John Paul II, in one of his catecheses on the person of Christ, made a similar declara-
tion: 'The first moment of the mystery of the Incarnation
of the Son of God is identified with the miraculous conception that took place by the power of the Holy Spirit
when Mary uttered her Yes.'[4]

These documents of the Magisterium echo the unan-
imous consensus of the Fathers. As a representative of
the Latins, we can invoke St Fulgentius of Ruspe (468–
533), who says simply that the virginal conception *was*
the taking of flesh, and that, therefore, 'no interval of time
can be reckoned between the beginning of the conceived
flesh and the arrival of the Majesty being conceived'.[5]
St John Damascene will serve as spokesman for the oriental tradition: 'As soon as there was flesh, it was flesh of
the Word, animated by a rational and intellectual soul.'[6]

The Annunciation: The Feast of the Incarnation

God the Son, fully and completely God, eternally begotten in the bosom of the Father, became fully and
completely man at his conception in the womb of the Virgin Mary. His human life began at fertilization, which in
his case was miraculous, because his Virgin Mother was
made fruitful, not by male seed, but by the power of the
Holy Spirit. That is why it is the Annunciation that is the

---

[3] *Epistola Synodica*; PG 87, 3161A. The relevant passage in the teaching of the eleventh Council of Toledo can be found at DS 534.

[4] *L'Osservatore romano* (July 2, 1987), 1.

[5] *Epistola XVII* 7; CCSL 91A, 568.

[6] *De Fide Orthodoxa* 3, 2; PG 94, 985C–988A.

chief feast of the Incarnation. The Nativity of Our Lord is also a celebration of the Incarnation but in a different sense. The Incarnation was effected in Nazareth and then manifested in Bethlehem. March 25 commemorates the moment of the enfleshing of the Word; December 25 commemorates his birth in the flesh taken nine months earlier. Christmas Day is a feast of 'theophany', a celebration, says St Gregory Nazianzen, of 'God manifested to man by birth'.[7] He comes forth from his Mother 'as a bridegroom out of his chamber or as the sun from his chamber to run his race' (cf. Ps 18:6). In the stable at Bethlehem, Mary can at last hold in her arms and feed at her breast, see with her own eyes, the Child-God who for nine months has been hidden in the hermitage of her womb. In the Byzantine liturgy, the Church sings with the voice of the Theotokos:

And she, bending over him like a handmaiden, worshipped him and said to him, as he lay in her arms: "How wast thou sown a seed in me? And how hast thou grown within me, O my Deliverer and my God?"[8]

On Christmas Day, in the company of Mary and Joseph and the shepherds, the meaning of the Incarnation seizes the mind and heart of the earthly Church: God, the Creator of the universe, has become a tiny baby. As St Bernard says, the Word was made 'infant flesh, young flesh, helpless flesh'.[9] But the Church also remembers, especially during the last week of Advent, that, before being a newborn baby, God incarnate was an unborn baby—in mod-

[7] *Oratio XXXVIII* 3; PG 36, 313C.
[8] Vespers for the Forefeast of the Nativity, *The Festal Menaion*, Eng. trans. (London, 1969), 202.
[9] *Sermo III in Nativitate Domini* 2; *Sancti Bernardi Opera*, vol. 4, ed. J. Leclercq and H. Rochais (Rome, 1966), 259.

ern jargon, a fetus, an embryo, a zygote. The first stage of human life that God made his own and thereby divinized was embryonic. The adventure of being human began for the eternal Son at the moment of his conception.

This dogmatic truth is proclaimed in the liturgies of both East and West on March 25. In the Roman Missal of Pope Paul VI, the celebration is a feast of the first rank (a 'solemnity') and is described as 'the Annunciation of the Lord'. During the Creed, at the '*Et incarnatus est*', the faithful are invited to kneel as a reminder of what the day commemorates. In the Byzantine rite, at Great Compline for 'The Annunciation of the Most Holy Theotokos and Ever-Virgin Mary', the Church sings these words:

> Let the heavens be glad and the earth rejoice: for the Son who is coeternal with the Father, having his throne and like him without beginning, in his compassion and merciful love for mankind has submitted himself to emptying (cf. Phil 2:7), according to the good pleasure and the counsel of the Father; and he has gone to dwell in a Virgin's womb that was sanctified beforehand by the Spirit. O marvel! God is come among men; he who cannot be contained is contained in a womb; the Timeless enters time; and strange wonder! His conception is without seed, his emptying is past telling; so great is this mystery! For God empties himself, takes flesh, and is fashioned as a creature, when the angel tells the pure Virgin of her conception: "Hail, thou who art full of grace; the Lord who has great mercy is with thee."[10]

---

[10] *The Festal Menaion*, Eng. trans. (London, 1969), 443f.

St Maximus the Confessor
on Christ's Human Beginning

If the mystery of man only becomes clear in the light of the Word Incarnate,[11] what does the moment of the Incarnation clarify? For St Maximus the Confessor (c. 580–662), it confirmed what he already believed on other grounds, namely, that the rational soul of man, which is not generated by his parents, is created immediately by God and infused into the body at the moment of conception (in modern jargon, the doctrine of 'immediate animation').

To assess the authority of this testimony, we must remember who St Maximus the Confessor was. Thanks to the pioneering work of Hans Urs von Balthasar, he is now generally recognized as the theological giant of the seventh century, the author of the crowning synthesis of Greek patristic theology and spirituality. (St John Damascene is among his legatees.) He is a second Athanasius, ready to withstand a whole empire in the defence of christological orthodoxy. He is a Byzantine through and through but also a loyal servant of the Pope of the elder Rome, a bridge between West and East. He is scholar but also monk and martyr, living and dying in the faith he preaches. 'This is the greatest example of that unity of doctrine and life that marks the whole patristic age; speculation and mysticism of the greatest subtlety are wedded to a soberly faced and consciously grasped martyrdom.'[12]

[11] *Gaudium et spes* 22; *Decreta*, 709.

[12] See Hans Urs von Balthasar, *Unser Auftrag: Bericht und Entwurf* (Einsiedeln, 1984), 36f. Balthasar here sums up the importance of Maximus in his own life and for the whole Church. In 1941 Balthasar wrote the first great work of modern Maximian scholarship. See the revised

The texts that most concern us come from the so-called 'Second *Ambigua*', in which Maximus (in response to the queries of John of Cyzicus) clears up obscurities in the writings of St Gregory Nazianzen. Origenist monks had given their own perverse reading. Maximus now offers an orthodox exegesis. One of the questions concerns the moment at which soul and body are united. Does the soul exist before the body (as the Origenists teach)? Or does the body exist before the intellectual soul (as Aristotle and the Stoics, in their different ways, teach)? Both hypotheses are to be rejected, says Maximus: the intellectual soul is created by God and infused into the body in the very instant of conception.

Building upon the work of St Gregory of Nyssa,[13] Maximus offers a number of arguments, philosophical and theological, but the decisive consideration, as we shall see, is christological.

Maximus insists that man is not a soul using a body but a unity of body and soul, a 'synthesis',[14] a 'complete figure' (*eidos holon*).[15] This 'completeness' (*ekplêrôsis*) of the human person enjoys a physical as well as metaphysical priority. If a man is essentially a whole, then he must be a whole from the beginning: the genesis of body and soul must be simultaneous. *This* soul is defined in relation to

---

second edition: *Kosmische Liturgie: Das Weltbild Maximus des Bekenners* (Einsiedeln, 1961). Balthasar's interpretation of Maximus is well discussed in W. Löser, *Im Geiste des Origines: Hans Urs von Balthasar als Interpret der Theologie der Kirchenväter* (Frankfurt, 1976), 181–212.

[13] St Gregory of Nyssa, *De hominis opificio* 28–29; PG 44, 229B–240B.

[14] *Ambigua* 2, 42; PG 91, 1324C.

[15] Ibid., 2, 7; 1101A. I am indebted to the fine article by M.-H. Congourdeau, 'L'Animation de l'embryon humain chez Maxime le Confesseur', *Nouvelle revue théologique* 111 (1989), 693–709.

this body; *that* body in relation to *that* soul. Each must, therefore, belong to the other from the outset. After all, even after separation in death, they do not lose their reference to each other. Maximus even suggests that, were soul not wedded to body from the beginning, there would be no reason why it should not, so to speak, divorce and remarry at the end: reincarnation would be as reasonable a human destiny as resurrection.

There is a quiet humour about some of Maximus' reasonings. He says that if the embryo immediately after fertilization is endowed with only a vegetative soul, then men father plants, not men. But in fact the act of fertilization establishes a human-to-human relationship between father and child; *I* am conceived by my father. Then again, Maximus says that he suspects that concealed behind the delayed animation theory is a Manichee distaste for any sort of association of the intellectual soul with the sordidness of sex.[16]

In Maximus' opinion, the strongest proof for the doctrine of immediate animation is the Incarnation.

> I regard nature's very maker, by the mystery of his Incarnation, to be the champion and infallible teacher of this doctrine. He truly became man and confirmed that he possessed the complete nature and existence [of man], subsisting in accordance with his coming into human existence. He inaugurated the renewal of nature, that is, conception by seed and birth through corruption, which human nature contracted after the transgression, when divine and spiritual increase degenerated into multitude.[17]

[16] *Ambigua* 2, 42; 1337B–1340B.
[17] Ibid., 1341BC. On St Gregory of Nyssa's arguments for 'immediate animation' see M. Canévet 'L'Humanité de l'embryon selon Grégoire de Nysse', *Nouvelle revue théologique* 114 (1992), 678–95.

Maximus applies to the Incarnation a distinction first used of the Trinity by the Cappadocians, namely, between 'definition of nature' (*logos tês physeôs*) and 'manner of existence' (*tropos tês hyparxeôs*).[18] It is the difference between *what* a thing is and does and *how* it is and does it. Maximus applies the distinction to Christ's conception. Its virginal and miraculous manner (by the direct operation of the Holy Spirit, without seed) does not make his human nature different from ours. In its 'definition of nature', Christ's humanity is the same as ours; it differs from ours only in the 'manner of its coming-to-be' (*tropos tês geneseôs*).

> By nature, [Christ's humanity] is the same [as ours], but, through the conception without seed (*asporia*), it is not the same, since this human nature was not that of a mere man but belonged to the One who for our sakes became man.[19]

The miraculous *how* of Christ's conception reveals *who* he is; it does not make him any the less *what* we are. This is the doctrine of Pope St Leo the Great (d. 461) in his *Tome*. The Son of God becomes man 'in a new order, generated in a new birth', but this newness—so 'singularly wonderful and wonderfully singular'—has not abolished the nature of our race.[20]

The newness of the virginal conception is the sign that here God is doing a new thing (cf. Is 43:19): he is becoming man to make all things new (cf. Rev 21:5). In an ordinary conception, a human person is thrown into

[18] On the *logos/tropos* distinction, see F. Heinzer, *Gottes Sohn als Mensch: Die Struktur des Menschseins Christi bei Maximus Confessor* (Freiburg, 1980), 171–81, 200ff.

[19] *Opuscula Theologica et Polemica* 4; PG 91, 60C.

[20] DS 292–94

existence through the 'urge of the flesh and the will of the male' (cf. Jn 1:13). He is one more son of Adam, come to swell the numbers of an ageing fallen 'multitude', with no other destiny but death. At the virginal conception, however, by the will of the Trinity, an eternally existing divine person, the only Son of the Father, becomes man to gather the scattered children of God into unity and bring them to the unageing newness of eternal life.

> The Word's birth for us in the flesh took place in a superior way to our own. Neither the will nor the thought of the passion-marked flesh preceded it, as happens in our case through the pleasure that has craftily made itself master of our birth. No, only the will of the Godhead preceded [the conception of Christ] through the Son who effected in himself his own Incarnation in fulfilment of the Father's loving plan and by the co-operation of the Holy Spirit. He thereby made new—in himself and by himself—the mode (*tropos*) of birth introduced into nature and accomplished the seedless conception in the Holy Mother of God and Ever-Virgin Mary.[21]

Apart from the saving novelty of its virginal manner, the conception of Christ is in all respects like ours. For us, then, as for him, it is the moment from which we are fully and completely human, endowed with rational soul as well as body.

Maximus' argument rests on his firm persuasion that the mystery of the hypostatic union of divinity and humanity in Christ is the key to understanding man, indeed, the whole created order. As Balthasar has shown, he makes the Chalcedonian dogma of 'union without confusion' a universal law of being, a fundamental axiom

---

[21] *Opuscula Theologica et Polemica* 20; PG 91, 240B.

of metaphysics.[22] The revealed doctrine of the Incarnation builds upon a naturally known philosophy of man, but it also contributes its own distinctive light and casts out the lingering shadows in man's self-understanding. The radiance of the virginal conception sheds its beams on every natural human conception. Through the Incarnation, man learns the truth about his beginnings.

Christ's Human Beginning and Ours: St Thomas Aquinas

Where Maximus saw a confirmation, Scholasticism found an exception: *unlike other men's*, Christ's body was animated by a rational soul at conception. The Schoolmen (following Aristotle) held the view that the rational soul is not infused at the first moment of conception but at a later time, that is, when the embryo has attained a sufficiently advanced state of bodily development.[23]

The philosophers of antiquity were not well up on the biology of modernity, and so they lacked the means (which we now have) of distinguishing an early human embryo from those of other species. To outward inspection, all embryos seemed to be of the same kind. The development, therefore, of a non-specific embryo into a recognizably human one had to be a process of substantial change—change of nature or form, change of *soul*. ('Soul' here means the form of the body, that which makes a body

---

[22] *Kosmische Liturgie: Das Weltbild Maximus des Bekenners*, 2d ed. (Einsiedeln, 1961), 57f.

[23] 'Where the Scholastics are forced to admit an exception from the law of successive forms—the mystery of Christ's Incarnation—Maximus finds a supreme confirmation of his own view' (*Kosmische Liturgie*, 173). Dante describes the Aristotelian-Scholastic embryology in the *Purgatorio* (25, 13–25).

to be the sort of body it is, its life-principle, the source of
its characteristic functions.) For Aristotle and St Thomas
Aquinas, human generation is a drama of transformation,
of 'coming to be' and 'passing away'.[24] At first, the embryo has a 'vegetative' soul: it is capable of nourishment
and growth. The vegetative soul 'passes away' and is succeeded by a soul that is both vegetative and sensitive: the
embryo is capable of sensation as well as nourishment.
Finally, the sensitive soul is replaced by one created directly by God, a soul that is at once vegetative, sensitive,
and rational: the embryo is alive with the life of man.[25]

St Thomas stood by this theory, not just because it
came to him from Aristotle, but because it corresponded
to what was observable in nature, and he was convinced
that a sound philosophy must be empirically based. 'The
judgement that the intellect makes concerning the nature
of a thing must conform to what sense perception shows
about the thing.'[26] Now the ancient world and the Middle
Ages knew nothing of ovulation; indeed, the ovum itself
was not discovered until 1827.[27] As far as St Thomas was
concerned, conception took place through the activation
by semen of a special secretion of blood in the womb.[28]
What is more, though he grasped the truth that matter
must be suitably and sufficiently organized in order to

[24] 'In man, as in other animals, one gets to the final form through
many generations and corruptions' (ST 1a 118, 2, ad 2).

[25] Cf. *Quaestiones de Anima* q. 11, ad 1; ST 1a 76, 3, ad 3; 118, 2, ad 2.
On the Aristotelian-Thomist view of the embryo, see Teresa Iglesias,
IVF and Justice. Moral, Social and Legal Issues Related to Human in vitro
Fertilization (London, 1990), 104ff.

[26] *In Librum Boethii de Trinitate Expositio* 6, 2.

[27] The discovery was made by Karl Ernst von Baer. See his *Epistola
de Ovo Mammalium et Hominis Genesi* (Leipzig, 1827).

[28] Cf. ST 3a 31, 5.

be animated by a rational soul, his judgement of what constituted organization was determined by the limitations of current observation. For Aristotle (and so for St Thomas), the soul is 'the primary act of a natural organic body' (*sômatos physikou organikou*), that is to say, a body with organs, parts serving some essential function.[29] Only when the embryonic body was equipped with recognizably human organs and limbs was it deemed to be alive with human life; when completely formed, it was evidently informed by a rational soul. Once there was the body of a man, there was a man, a rational animal.

St Thomas taught that Christ's body did not develop in the normal manner. Having been created directly by the Holy Spirit from the flesh and blood of the Virgin, without any involvement of male seed, it was fully formed, perfectly organized, from the first moment of conception, and from that first moment was animated by a rational soul.[30] St Bonaventure held the same opinion: from his conception, Christ's body had 'perfection of organization'.[31]

There is an obvious difficulty with this opinion. If the incarnate Word is to be called 'man' univocally, why should he differ from other men with regard to the animation of his human body? In the terminology of St Maximus, it would seem to imply a difference in the 'definition of nature' rather than the 'manner of existence'. St Thomas considers this question in an objection quoting St Leo the Great.[32] He replies that the difference be-

---

[29] *De Anima* 2, 1; 412B.

[30] ST 3a 33, 1 and 2.

[31] *Commentarius in III Librum Sententiarum*, d. 3, p. 2, a. 3, q. 2; *Opera Omnia Sancti Bonaventurae*, vol. 3 (Quaracchi, 1887), 93.

[32] ST 3a 33, 2, ad 1.

tween Christ and us in this respect is one of timing, not of nature. Our Lord's animation was essentially the same as other men's in the sense that his rational soul, like all others, was infused as soon as the body was formed. What was different was the time of that formation: Christ's body was perfectly formed at an earlier moment than other men's.

Were he alive today, St Thomas would without doubt hold the doctrine of immediate animation. The fundamental principles of his philosophy of man are independent of his obsolete biology; indeed, when applied to modern knowledge, they provide formidable support for immediate animation. Stripping off the shell of the out-of-date science, we find the permanently valid kernel of his thought on the soul. This is not wishful thinking. It is simply the application of the Thomist axiom stated earlier: philosophy must have an empirical base.

The essential principles of Thomist anthropology are as follows:

A. *The soul is not the self.* A man is not only a soul but something composed of soul and body.[33] The soul separated from the body is not a man.[34] The soul on its own can no more be called a person than a hand or foot on its own. The person is the possessor of the *complete* nature of the species.[35]

B. *It is natural for the soul to be united to the body.* That is why the separation of soul from body at death is 'against nature' and why the resurrection of the body is in a certain sense 'necessary'.[36]

[33] Ibid., 1a 75, 4.
[34] Ibid.; cf. 3a 50, 4.
[35] Ibid., 1a 75, 4, ad 2; cf. 1a 29, 1, ad 5.
[36] Ibid., 1a 118, 3; *Summa Contra Gentiles* 3, 79.

C. *The soul is the form of the body.*[37] 'Form' here means the innermost shaping principle of a thing, making it to be what it is. The soul is not a motor in a machine, making it move. No, it is what makes the body what it is, the body of a man. An ensouled body is the body of a living human being.

D. *The rational soul, which is not transmitted by the parents, is infused by God as soon as the body is ready to receive it.*[38] It must be suitably organized. St Thomas explains how the human body is suitably disposed by the Divine Artist for those spiritual acts of which only man among bodily creatures is capable. His senses are not just for food and sex but for knowledge, and so he does not sniff around on the ground but stands upright and can lift up his face to contemplate the heavens.[39]

Modern biology has proved that the fundamental 'disposition' or 'organization' of living matter is genetic (cf. D). We can now do what the ancients could not: we can distinguish the human embryo from embryos of other species. The perceptible form of the zygote, its genetic structure, may therefore be regarded as, so to speak, the outward and visible sign of its metaphysical form, that which makes it to be what it is, a member of the human species (cf. C). 'The human zygote as we understand it today with DNA and RNA would in Thomas' understanding eminently satisfy as having the organized matter required for the infusion of a human spiritual soul.'[40]

[37] ST 1a 91, 4, ad 3.
[38] Ibid., 1a 100, 1, ad 2.
[39] Ibid., 1a 91, 3, ad 3.
[40] J. T. Mangan, S.J., 'The Wonder of Myself: Ethical-Theological Aspects of Direct Abortion', *Theological Studies* (1970), 129f. The distinguished German pathologist, Franz Büchner, has written: 'By the

Thus man is a natural and complete whole from his conception (cf. A and B). The embryo is alive with unmis-
takably human life. For St Thomas, that is just another
way of saying that it is ensouled with a human (rational)
soul. 'It' is already 'he' or 'she'.

The doctrine of immediate animation makes St Thomas'
Christology shine with even greater power. It resolves
tensions and unanswered questions.

   1. The Angelic Doctor tells us that, while Our Lord's
conception was wholly miraculous in the sense that its
active principle was the supernatural power of the Holy
Spirit (rather than the natural power of male seed), it was
wholly natural when we consider the matter furnished
by his Mother.⁴¹ Strictly, on St Thomas' view, one ought
to add that the conception was also, if not miraculous,
at least extraordinary in the sense that his body was ani-

---

equipment of its cell nucleus with a new combination of maternal and
paternal DNA, [the fertilized ovum] represents a new creation such as
never existed before. . . . Modern biology and pathology just will not
allow us to mark off . . . certain sections of embryonic development
as pre-human or not yet specifically human stages. We must rather in-
creasingly learn, despite the apparent insignificance and smallness of the
first stages of human development, to integrate wholly into our picture
of man the potentialities and plenitude of its vital expressions as they
gradually unfold and recognize the human embryonic stage as one of
the great periods of human existence, with childhood, maturity, and
the form of life proper to old age. In other words, we must see human
life as a temporal configuration, in Guardini's sense, in which from
conception till death there is neither a "not yet" nor a "no longer" '
('Development of the Embryo and Human Ontogenesis', *International
Catholic Review* 1 [1972], 306. See also Michael Allyn Taylor's doctoral
dissertation, *Human Generation in the Thought of Thomas Aquinas: A Case
Study on the Role of Biological Fact in Theological Science* [Washington, D.C.:
Catholic University of America, 1982]).

⁴¹ ST 3a 33, 4.

mated at an earlier moment than any other human body. If, however, Christ is like us even in the moment of his animation, then we can appreciate the sense in which, though in its manner it is miraculous, his conception remains completely natural, the beginning of real and complete human life.

2. If the Son of God's embryonic condition is like that of every other human being, we understand better what St Thomas has to say about his self-emptying and his assumption of our 'natural and blameless disabilities'.[42] He emptied himself, not by laying aside his divine greatness, but by taking on our human littleness, and first of all the microscopic infirmity of the embryo. He accepts the limitations of the long, slow womb-way to birth. Apart from the virginal manner of his conception and birth, the Christ Child, unborn as well as newborn, is like every baby.[43]

3. St Thomas' doctrine of man is undoubtedly christocentric. He does not confuse philosophy with theology, truths of natural philosophy with truths of supernatural revelation, but his faith in God-made-man does give added weight to what his reason tells him of man-made-by-God. As Josef Pieper says:

> Thomas might never have had the courage to defend natural and visible reality, in particular man's corporeality, as an essential part of man and would never have had the courage to draw the ultimate conclusions from this conviction had he not thought in terms of the Incarnation of God. . . . One who believes that the Logos of God has, in

[42] On the meaning of Christ's self-emptying, see St Thomas Aquinas, *Super Epistolam S. Pauli Apostoli ad Philippenses* cap. 2, lectio 2. On the 'natural and blameless passions', see ST 3a 14, 4.

[43] ST 3a 29, 1, ad 3.

Christ, united with the bodily nature of man cannot possibly assume at the same time that the material reality is not good. And how can visible things be evil if the "medicine of salvation" deriving from that prototypal Sacrament be offered to man in the same visible things . . . when the sacraments are performed.[44]

As a general principle, this is certainly true. In the *Summa Theologiae*, anthropology is presented in a christological (and trinitarian) frame. Man (at the end of the first part and throughout the second part) is enveloped by the one Lord Jesus Christ: in the mysteries of his divinity (in the first part) and in the mysteries of his humanity (in the third part). St Thomas looks at the human person

[44] J. Pieper, *Introduction to Thomas Aquinas*, Eng. trans. (London, 1963), 13. The great Dominican scholar, M.-D. Chenu, O.P., would appear to challenge our interpretation: 'The Incarnation is, however, in point of fact, a contingent event, and it enters in the *exitus-reditus* cycle only as an absolutely gratuitous work of God's absolutely free will. The predestination of Christ is *de facto* capital, yet it does not have its place by dint of right in the economy of this cycle. It is impossible to locate it *a priori* in a dialectical list of divine decrees' (*Toward Understanding St Thomas*, Eng. trans. [Chicago, 1964], 314). This statement makes the mistake, so it seems to me, of assuming that the *Summa* could be christocentric only on the supposition of the absolute predestination of the Incarnation, a view that, of course, St Thomas does not hold (cf. ST 3a 1, 3). In fact, another kind of christocentricity is possible and, in my opinion, is to be found in the *Summa*, that is to say, one built upon the actualities of saving history—of the sin of Adam and man's need of redemption. See my book *The Christocentricity of Pope John Paul II* (forthcoming). The *exitus-reditus* movement of the *Summa* is not only philosophical and abstract: it is also historical and concrete. It corresponds to the drama of saving history: man's creation in the image of God (*Prima Pars*); his fall (*Prima Secundae*) and need for redeeming grace (ibid.); the Law (ibid.) and the Prophets (*Secunda Secundae*); man's redemption by Jesus Christ, the 'way to God' (*Tertia Pars*).

in the light of the divine person of the Word-made-flesh.
Only with respect to the moment of animation does the
principle appear to have been inconsistently applied.

II

HOW CAN THE ARK OF THE LORD
COME TO ME? THE GOSPELS

The first place in which we find Jesus in the Gospels is the womb of Mary—in her 'innermost parts', say Matthew and Luke with energetic realism (*en gastri, en tê koilia*, Mt 1:18; Lk 1:31; 2:21). He is not only the inhabitant of the womb; he is also its 'fruit' (cf. Lk 1:42). His body does not come down from heaven; it is fashioned out of his Virgin Mother's flesh and blood. Indeed, since she is made fruitful by the Holy Spirit, not by male seed (cf. Mt 1:20), he is physically more indebted to her than any other child could be to his mother. Moreover, since in the Bible the bodily is the sacrament of the spiritual, Mary's enfolding of Christ in her womb is preceded by her soul's assent (cf. 1:38), accompanied by her spirit's rejoicing (cf. 1:46–55), and followed by her heart's contemplation (cf. 2:19; 2:51). She gives him his humanity in faith and love.[1]

Apart from the journey to Bethlehem, St Luke records only one event during Our Lady's pregnancy: the Visitation. 'In those days', after the departure of Gabriel, Mary hastened to visit her cousin Elizabeth in the hill country of Judaea (cf. 1:39f.), probably in the neighbourhood of Ain-Karim, six kilometres to the west of Jerusalem. The evangelist says that, in going south, Mary 'arose'

[1] René Laurentin, *The Truth of Christmas beyond the Myths: The Gospels of the Infancy of Christ*, Eng. trans. (Petersham, 1986), 127.

(*anastasa*), the verb used to designate the Resurrection.
This strong and suggestive word, one of Luke's favourites,
heightens the drama of Mary's journey: it is an ascent, a
climb into the high country. The same language is used to
report the three other southward expeditions of Jesus and
Mary (2:4, 22, and 42).[2] It is as if Luke wants Theophilus
to lift up his eyes to the mountains (cf. Ps 120:1), to the
heights of Mount Zion. Later, he will show how, in his
public ministry, Jesus kept his sights on Jerusalem: 'When
the days drew near for him to be received up, he set his
face to go to Jerusalem' (9:51). The message of Luke 1:39
is that the first time the Saviour ventured south, presaging
his later journey, was as an unborn child. Mary carries
Jesus on the road that later he will purposefully tread.

There is irony in the topography. The lofty earthly
Jerusalem is later to fall (cf. Lk 21:20ff.; 23:28ff.). It
kills first the prophets and finally the Son (cf. Lk 13:34).
And, though the last fully recorded episode in the infancy
Gospel takes place in the Temple, the religious establish-
ment is dumbfounded by the Child-God, and the evangelist quietly closes the narrative with the statement that
Jesus *went down* to lowly Nazareth, there humbly to obey
his parents (cf. 2:51). Jerusalem does not have the last
word. It is being superseded. A new and greater Temple
is here.

The chief actors in the drama of the Visitation are two
babes in the womb, Jesus in Mary, John in Elizabeth,
the Prince and the Prophet, the Word and the Voice.[3]
Luke says that the unborn Baptist 'skipped' (*eskirtêsen*)

[2] Ibid., 122.

[3] In the Ambrosian Missal, in the entrance antiphon for the feast
of the Visitation, we hear Elizabeth addressing Mary: 'You carry the
Prince, I the Prophet, you the Giver of the Law, I the Receiver of the

in his mother's womb when she heard the greeting of the Christ-carrying Virgin (cf. 1:41). Elizabeth is overwhelmed. Her baby's inward dance—he jumps 'for joy', says Elizabeth, *en agalliasei* (v. 44)—fills her with the Holy Spirit. She recognizes her cousin's unborn baby, the blessed fruit of her womb, as God, 'my Lord' (cf. v. 43),[4] and declares Mary to be 'blessed among women', blessed in body and in soul, blessed because of the One she carries, blessed because she believed (v. 45).

Later in life, John will point out Jesus as Messiah and Lamb of God (cf. Mt 3:1–12; Jn 1:6f., 15f., 19–36; 3:22–30ff.). Luke backdates his work of witness to the womb.[5] Even unborn, John is Christ's herald; by his infant joy, he is prophet. As St Ambrose says, 'before his father or mother had done anything wonderful, he leapt in his mother's womb and preached the good news of the advent of the Lord.'[6] St Augustine is even of the opinion that the unborn Baptist was miraculously endowed with the use of reason and will so that he could joyfully recognize, believe in and say Yes to his Lord.[7]

Some exegetes, modern as well as patristic and me-

Law, you the Word, I the Voice proclaiming the Saviour's coming' (*Missale Ambrosianum* [Milan, 1924], 418).

[4] The *Glossa Ordinaria* paraphrases St Elizabeth's words (Lk 1:43) as follows: 'I sense a miracle. I recognize a miracle: the Mother of the Lord, pregnant with the Word, full of God' (PL 114, 247C).

[5] 'The first meeting of Jesus and the Baptist takes place in the blessed wombs of the two mothers-to-be' (Heinz Schürmann, *Das Lukasevangelium*, Erster Teil [Freiburg, Basel, and Vienna, 1969], 66).

[6] St Ambrose, *Expositio Evangelii secundum Lucam* 1, 33; CCSL 14, 22f.

[7] *Epistola* CLXXXVII, 7, 24; PL 33, 841. St Augustine emphasizes that this is a truly miraculous recognition. He is not suggesting that the

dieval, have suggested that John's merry dance has affinities with the matrimonial symbolism of Old and New Testaments.[8] By exulting in the womb, John shows himself to be that 'best man' who rejoices when he hears the Bridegroom's voice (cf. Jn 3:29). And the divine Bridegroom himself, borne within his Mother, 'leaps upon the mountains' and, through her voice, announces to John, Elizabeth, and all mankind that the winter of sin and death is over (cf. Song 2:8ff.).[9] Spring comes with the spring of the newly conceived Redeemer.

The God-Man sanctified his forerunner while they were both being carried by their mothers. At the Visitation, the promise made to Zechariah comes true: '[John] will be filled with the Holy Spirit even from his mother's womb' (1:15). The grace of the Holy Spirit flows from Jesus through Mary to John and from John to Elizabeth. Origen (c. 185–c. 254) describes this cascade of the Spirit, this proto-Pentecost, as follows:

> Jesus, who was in [Mary's] womb, hurried to sanctify John still in his mother's womb. Before Mary arrived and greeted Elizabeth, the child had not leapt in the womb, but as soon as Mary had spoken the word that the Son of God

---

infant Baptist's behaviour should be taken as a 'norm for what is to be thought of babies' (ibid.).

[8] Cf. St Bonaventure, *In Lucam* 1, 41; *Sancti Bonaventurae Opera Omnia* 7 (Quaracchi, 1895), 28 (n. 76). On the interconnection of Song of Songs 2:8–14, Lk 1:39–45, and John 3:29ff., see A. Feuillet, *Jésus et sa mère: D'après les récits lucaniens de l'enfance et d'après St Jean* (Paris, 1974), 25f.

[9] As the *Glossa Ordinaria* says, 'He made a leap from heaven into the womb, from the womb into the manger, from the manger to the Cross, from the Cross to the tomb, from the tomb he returned to heaven' (PL 113, 1138D–1139A).

in her womb had suggested, the child leapt with joy, and
at that moment Jesus made his precursor his prophet. . . .
There is no doubt that she who was then filled with the
Holy Spirit was filled on account of her son. She was
not the first to be granted the Holy Spirit. No, only when
John, enclosed in her womb, had received the Holy Spirit,
only after his sanctification, was she filled with the Holy
Spirit. . . .[10]

Even before his birth, the Child Jesus is at his saving,
sanctifying work. While still in the womb, the Saviour
consecrates the forerunner for his mission. What is more,
grace comes to John from Jesus *through Mary*, who, in
Gerard Manley Hopkins' words, 'this one work has to do
—Let all God's glory through.'[11] Already, at Ain-Karim,
Mary is at her handmaidenly, motherly work of mediat-
ing the grace of her Son.

The Ark of the Covenant

There is good reason for thinking that St Luke's description of Jesus-in-Mary's journey to Elizabeth was intended
by the evangelist to recall the transfer of the Ark of the
Covenant to Jerusalem (cf. 2 Sam 6).[12] The wonder in

[10] Origen, *Homilia VIII in Lucam*; ed. M. Rauer (Berlin, 1959), 41ff.
The phrase 'proto-Pentecost' comes from René Laurentin, 99. Pope
John Paul II adds this insight: 'Mother and son are united in a kind
of spiritual symbiosis, by which the exultation of the baby almost in-
fects her who conceived him, and behold, Elizabeth breaks out into
that shout which expresses the joy that she profoundly shared with her
son, as Luke testifies' (*L'Osservatore romano*, English edition [June 18,
1990], 5).
[11] 'The Blessed Virgin Compared to the Air We Breathe', *The Poetical
Works of Gerard Manley Hopkins*, ed. Norman H. Mackenzie (Oxford,
1990), 173.
[12] Cf. R. Laurentin, *Structure et théologie de Luc 1–2* (Paris, 1957), 73ff.

Elizabeth's words of welcome match the awe of David when he receives the Ark:

> And why is this granted me, that the Mother of my Lord should come to me? (Lk 1:43)

> How can the Ark of the Lord come to me? (2 Sam 6:9)

✳ The Ark, like Mary, travels up into the Judaean hills (cf. 2 Sam 6:2; Lk 1:39). The transfer, like the Visitation, is an occasion of delight (cf. 2 Sam 6:12; Lk 1:44). David the King 'leaps and dances before the Lord' (2 Sam 6:16); so does John the Baptist (cf. Lk 1:44). The Ark remains in the house of Obededom for three months (2 Sam 6:11); Mary stays with Elizabeth 'for about three months' (Lk 1:56). The inexactness in the chronology is important. It shows that Luke's intention is the reporting of historical facts (cf. Lk 1:2), not the inventing of symbolic stories.

> The word 'about' (*hôs*) brings home to us his respect for historical facts. He has without doubt rounded the number off for the sake of the coincidence. But he has taken scrupulous care to inform us of what he is doing. He may stylize, but he does not invent.[13]

The Incarnate Presence of God

The Babe in the womb is God, so the expectant Mother is the definitive Ark, the antitypical shrine and sanctuary of the divine presence. That is what the Visitation narrative implies, as do the two contrasting annunciations that precede it. When the angel appears to Zechariah the Priest to announce the Baptist's birth, he visits him in the place of his cultic duties, in the Temple, amid the swirl

---

[13] Ibid., 81.

of incense (cf. Lk 1:8ff.). The scene is painted in sacerdo-
tal scarlet and gold, in the style of Rubens. But Gabriel
brings his glad tidings to Mary in her own home: 'Mary
is "substituted for the sanctuary" '.[14] The palate is more
modest, the peasant hues of a Rembrandt. The angel does
not place himself, with rubrical correctness, 'on the right
side of the altar of incense' (cf. 1:11). He just 'comes to
her' and speaks (cf. v. 28). The Virgin Theotokos, simple laywoman that she is, is greater than any priest, more
exalted than any man-made temple.

Gabriel's words about Mary's 'overshadowing' by the
'Power of the Most High' would recall to any Jewish
mind the 'Shekinah' of Yahweh, the word coined by post-
biblical Judaism for the divine presence, epitomized so often in the past by a dazzling nimbus: the cloud covering
the summit of Sinai from which the Lord speaks to Moses
(cf. Ex 24:15–18); the pillar of cloud, thick and gloomy by
day, clear and bright by night, which guided the Israelites
on their journey through the wilderness; the cloud that
settled over the tent of meeting (cf. Ex 40:34); and the
cloud filling the Temple when Solomon consecrates it
(cf. 2 Chron 5:13).[15] There can be only one conclusion:
God is making himself present in Mary.

The cloud is an ambiguous image of presence: a visible
pledge but also a darkening cover, a fitting outward sign,
therefore, of both the immanence and transcendence of
God. 'The Shekinah, even while giving itself to man,
eludes his grasp. . . . The *Deus revelatus* reveals himself as
the *Deus absconditus*.'[16] The Jews yearned for the assur-

[14] R. Laurentin, *The Truth of Christmas*, 123.

[15] Cf. I. de la Potterie, *Marie dans le mystère de l'alliance* (Paris, 1988),
64.

[16] L. Bouyer, *La Bible et l'Évangile: Le Sens de l'Écriture: du Dieu qui

ance of God's nearer presence, but just as ardently they insisted that he was 'wholly other'. When he dedicates the Temple, Solomon recognizes that 'heaven and the highest heaven' cannot contain the Lord his God, but he prays nonetheless that the divine *name* may be set in the sanctuary (1 Kings 8:28ff.; 2 Chron 6:18ff.).[17] The Incarnation fulfilled the longing for immanence beyond all Jewish expectation and at the same time confirmed the Old Testament's reverence for God's transcendence. For, in the womb of the Virgin, the coeternal Son assumes the true nature of man while remaining transcendent true God. Without ceasing to be uncircumscribable in his divinity, he becomes—without seed, by the power of the Holy Spirit alone—a tiny human embryo, contained by the walls of a virginal womb. The Incarnation is not the degradation of divine greatness but the elevation of human littleness through its assumption by the Creator. And so through Mary, by her faith and in her body, Israel's longing for God to rend the heavens and come down is

---

parle au Dieu fait homme (Paris, 1951), 108–10. Balthasar says that the Incarnation fulfils 'in a superabundant manner what God himself had introduced into Israel: the fact that, in his own Word, spoken into history and into the heart of the people, he explains himself to them ever more deeply and abandons himself to them ever more defencelessly, and that precisely in this manner he reveals himself more and more as he who remains inconceivably concealed. All particular considerations aside, the Incarnation of the Word means the most extreme manifestness within the deepest concealment' (*The Glory of the Lord: A Theological Aesthetics*, vol. 1: *Seeing the Form*, Eng. trans. [Edinburgh, 1982], 457).

[17] On the 'name' theology of the Deuteronomistic writers, see M. Weinfeld, *Deuteronomy and the Deuteronomic School* (Oxford, 1972), 191–209.

fulfilled. The incomprehensible God dwells among men as a man.

God in the Midst of Daughter Zion

The later prophets, inspired by the Spirit, addressed God's people as if 'it' were 'she'—a single person, a young girl, the Virgin Daughter of Zion, and they looked forward to her future restoration, when God would be 'in her midst' (cf. Zeph 3:14–17; Zech 2:10).[18] The Targum (the first-century A.D. Aramaic translation) of these two texts introduces in both a reference to the Shekinah: 'I will make my Shekinah dwell in your midst.'[19] That hope for God's 'central' presence is fulfilled in Mary with a realism beyond any prophet's dream. 'Highly favoured' from her Immaculate Conception by the grace of the Holy Spirit, she stands before the Father's angel as the perfect realization of Daughter Zion, the representative of her people and indeed of all mankind, and in faith and love she gives human nature to the coeternal Son. Now indeed does God dwell on earth (cf. 1 Kings 8:27), as flesh of Mary's flesh and in her womb, 'in the midst' of her body, 'in her innermost parts' (*en gastri*).[20]

This New Testament revelation of Jesus in Mary pre-

[18] See N. Lemmo, 'Maria, "Figlia di Sion", a partire da Lc 1, 26–38. Bilancio esegetico dal 1939 a 1982', *Marianum* 45 (1983), 175–258; and de la Potterie, 20ff.

[19] *The Targum of the Minor Prophets*. Translated, with a critical introduction, appendix, and notes by K. J. Cathcart and R. P. Gordon (Edinburgh, 1989), 173 and 189. According to the editors of this translation, the Shekinah concept enables the Targumists 'to express the truth of God's presence among his people without prejudice to the ultimate truth of his transcendence' (4).

[20] Laurentin, *The Truth of Christmas*, 123.

supposes the Old Testament belief that the womb of woman is the stage on which the first scenes of the human drama are played out. The Lord forms, 'knits together', every man from the womb (cf. 2 Macc 7:22f.; Ps 138:13ff.; Is 44:2, 24). Indeed, 'He-who-fashions-you-in-the-womb' is one of the divine names in Deutero-Isaiah (cf. 49:5). The nakedness of the human person as he comes from the womb foreshadows the nakedness with which he goes into the tomb: both signal his utter dependence upon his Creator (cf. Job 1:21). The biographies of Israel's fathers begin with their conception: Isaac (Gen 21:2), Jacob (Gen 25:21), Moses (Ex 2:2), Samuel (1 Sam 1:20). Womb conduct prefigures adult character, as the struggle of the unborn Esau and Jacob proves (cf. Gen 25:22). Jeremiah is consecrated to his prophetic mission before his birth: 'Before I formed you in the womb I knew you, and before you were born I consecrated you; I appointed you a prophet to the nations' (Jer 1:5). Deutero-Isaiah, too, had been 'appointed' ever since he 'lay in the womb' (Knox 49:5). Some of the Rabbis believed that the unborn child had sometimes been miraculously made capable of religious acts. According to Rabban Gamaliel II (c. 90), when Israel crossed the Red Sea, 'even the embryos in their mothers' wombs sang a song.'[21] Thus in Mary, who conceives her Son by the

---

[21] Strack-Billerbeck *Kommentar zum Neuen Testament aus Talmud und Midrasch*, 2 (Munich, 1924), 101. 'The tradition frequently and emphatically shows how the Baptist pointed to Jesus. . . . Here this witness of John's to Jesus is backdated to his mother's womb. This is in line with the Jewish view that a person's adult life is foreshadowed in his behaviour when unborn in the womb (cf. Gen 25:22f.)' (Heinz Schürmann, *Das Lukasevangelium*, Erster Teil [Freiburg, Basel, and Vienna, 1969], 67).

Holy Spirit, not by human seed, two major themes of
the Old Testament converge and are surpassed—the hidden presence of God and the secret beginnings of man.

The Pregnant Mother's Praise

At the close of the Visitation narrative, the pregnant
Mary praises God in the Magnificat. St Bede the Venera-
ble (673–735), Northumbrian Father and Doctor of the
Church, offers this gloss: 'My spirit rejoices in the eternal
divinity of Jesus, that is, the Saviour, whom I have conceived in time and bear in my flesh.'[22] In our own times,
for a century and a half, radical biblical criticism has tried
to wrest this incomparable song from Mary. Authorship
has been transferred to Elizabeth and Zechariah. It is al-
leged to be a cento of Old Testament texts assembled by
the evangelist, a Maccabean psalm, or a post-Resurrection
Christian hymn. In a breathtaking display of unscientific
prejudgement, Raymond Brown has declared that it is
'unlikely that such finished poetry could have been composed on the spot by ordinary people'.[23] (A visit to the
public houses of North Wales, where 'ordinary people'
improvise 'finished poetry' in the strict metres of classical Welsh verse, would be a suitable penance for Father
Brown!) The theories are mutually exclusive and have
nothing but implausibility in common. The Magnificat
is not Luke's work; he inherited it. Its semitisms suggest
a Palestinian provenance. Moreover, the fact that it is a
personal hymn of thanksgiving requires a specific occasion of gratitude.

[22] St Bede, *In Lucam* 1, 46; CCSL 120, 37.
[23] R. E. Brown, *The Birth of the Messiah: A Commentary on the Infancy
Narratives in Matthew and Luke* (London, 1977), 346.

Neither in Jewish circles nor in the early Christian communities could an appropriate *Sitz-im-Leben* for a psalm of this kind be assigned: in its fundamental assertions, it fits nowhere better than in Mary's situation.[24]

The transportation of the Magnificat on the stream of oral tradition has doubtless smoothed and streamlined the text finally written down. 'But to transmit is not to create.'[25] Mary's hymn was handed down by men and women raised in a religious culture that prized faithfulness of memory and resisted the imagination's propensity to embellish.[26] Luke indicates not only the source of the infancy narratives but the method of their transmission when he twice refers to Mary's treasuring memory (cf. Lk 2:19, 51). The resemblances to the song of Hannah, Samuel's mother (cf. 1 Sam 2:1-10) and to the Psalms (especially the references to the poor, the *anawim*, God's favourites), confirm, rather than weaken, the source of the song in Mary. Nothing is more typically oriental and Jewish than the use of traditional verse for the expression of joy or sorrow.[27] As we now know from the Dead Sea

[24] Heinz Schürmann, *Das Lukasevangelium*, 79.

[25] Laurentin, *The Truth of Christmas*, 381.

[26] For the Rabbis, memorizing played a key role in the assimilation of the Torah. 'The material that must be known is *memorized*. It is imprinted on the memory ready formulated and is kept alive by constant repetition. It is carried on the lips. . . . The study of the Torah is, according to a typical mode of expression "a work of the *mouth*", and they call the mouth blessed for having been created as a receptacle for the Torah' (Birger Gerhardsson, *Memory and Manuscript: Oral Tradition and Written Transmission in Rabbinic Judaism and Early Christianity*, Eng. trans. [Uppsala, 1961], 81).

[27] 'From childhood the Jews knew many of the Old Testament lyrics by heart; and just as our own poor, who know no literature but the Bible, easily fall into biblical language in times of special joy or sor-

Scrolls, in the Palestinian Judaism of the first century, there were many godly folk who knew the Scriptures almost by heart.[28] They could, therefore, draw on them spontaneously to express, in an attitude of faith, all the feelings of their heart.

> It is therefore reasonable to suppose that the same was true of the Virgin Mary. Hearing the Word of God each week in the synagogue, she did not cease, in wonder, to make comparisons between the ancient oracles and what had happened to her personally. It is this wonderment of Mary that St Luke's infancy narratives try to communicate to us.[29]

Nothing could be more Jewish than a set of 'variations on a theme by Hannah' composed by her daughter-in-faith, Mary of Nazareth, in joyful celebration of the Messiah's presence in her womb. The Magnificat has its ultimate source in the heart and lips of Mary, not in the mind and pen of Luke.

> Mary in that moment felt welling up from the depths of her soul the verses of the canticle of Anna, Samuel's mother (cf. 1 Sam 2:1–10), as well as other Old Testament verses, in order to give free expression to the feelings of the "Daughter of Zion", which found highest fulfilment in her. That is what the evangelist came to know so well, on the basis of the private conversation that he directly or indirectly shared with Mary. Among what was passed on

---

row, so Mary would naturally fall back on the familiar expressions of Jewish Scripture in this moment of intense exultation' (A. Plummer, *A Critical and Exegetical Commentary on the Gospel according to St Luke*, 4th ed. [Edinburgh, 1901], 30).

[28] See A. Feuillet, *Jésus et sa mère*, 82.

[29] Ibid., 83.

there must have been news of that joy that the two mothers shared in common during that meeting, as the fruit of the love that beat in their hearts. It was the trinitarian Spirit-Love, who was revealing himself on the threshold of the "fullness of time" (Gal 4:4), inaugurated in the mystery of the Incarnation of the Word. Already in that blessed moment what Paul would later say was being fulfilled: "The fruit of the Holy Spirit . . . love, joy, peace" (Gal 5:22).[30]

If the Annunciation narrative reveals the faith and love with which the Virgin welcomed God's Son into her flesh, the Magnificat reveals the joy and gratitude with which she sheltered him. These religious acts are more than simply individual. Mary of the Magnificat is Israel in person. Her 'I' recapitulates the 'we' of her people. What God has done for her, he has done for all Israel (cf. 1:54). The grace poured out on the lowly Handmaid is a blessing for all the poor of Yahweh (cf. vv. 48 and 53). In the Child in Mary's womb, every promise made to Abraham is fulfilled (cf. v. 55).

The Magnificat marks an unprecedented moment in salvation history. Israel's expectation has become an expectant mother's longing. Prophets, priests, and princes praised and hoped in God, but their dedication was flawed and incomplete. Now, by the grace that fills her from her conception, the Messiah-bearing Maiden brings all Israel's faith, hope, and love to its finest flourishing, gives it undefiled expression. The supreme religious acts of the Old Law are not masculine and priestly but feminine and motherly. For nine months, the purest worship, the humblest prayer, is a Mother's devotion to the Child within her body. And this marvellous end of the Old is also the

[30] Ibid., 82.

beginning of the New. The Blessed Virgin is more than just the culmination of Israel, she is also the beginning of the Church, the Church's model in faith and charity and union with Christ.[31] Thus, according to St Irenaeus, 'in her exultation she prophetically declared in the name of the Church, "My soul magnifies the Lord . . ."'.[32] Each evening the Church sings Magnificat, so that, as they hasten through the hills of history, her members may share a little of Our Lady's devotion to Christ. Like the Holy Theotokos, and with her help, they try in all things 'to magnify the Lord and to rejoice in God our Saviour'.

The Guardian of the Shrine

St Matthew's account of Our Lady's pregnancy has at its centre the figure of St Joseph. The Catholic Revised Standard Version translates the passage as follows:

> Now the birth of Jesus Christ took place in this way. When his mother had been betrothed to Joseph, before they came together she was found to be with child of the Holy Spirit; and her husband Joseph, being a just man and unwilling to put her to shame, resolved to send her away quietly. But as he considered this, behold, an angel of the Lord appeared to him in a dream, saying, "Joseph, son of David, do not fear to take Mary your wife, for that which is conceived in her is of the Holy Spirit; she will bear a son, and you shall call his name Jesus, for he will save his people from their sins." All this took place to fulfil what the Lord had spoken by the prophet: "Behold, a virgin shall conceive and bear a son, and his name shall be

---

[31] *Lumen Gentium* 63 and 68; *Decreta*, 201 and 205; cf. the preface to the Mass for *Beata Maria Virgo, Electa Israel Progenies, Collectio Missarum de Beata Maria Virgine* I (Vatican City, 1987), 7.

[32] *Adversus Haereses* 3, 10, 2; SC 34, 164.

called Emmanuel" (which means "God with us"). When
Joseph woke from sleep, he did as the angel of the Lord
commanded him; he took his wife, but knew her not until
she had borne a son; and he called his name Jesus (Mt
1:18–25).

It is possible, without distortion, to translate these same
verses with a different emphasis:

> Now the origin of Jesus as Messiah is as follows. When
> his mother Mary had been betrothed to Joseph, before
> they came together, she was found to be with child by
> the power of the Holy Spirit; and her husband Joseph,
> being a holy man and not wanting to reveal her mystery,
> resolved to withdraw from her quietly. But when he had
> formed this plan, behold, an angel of the Lord appeared to
> him in a dream, saying, "Joseph, son of David, do not fear
> to take Mary as your wife, for her child has indeed been
> conceived by the Holy Spirit; she will bear a son, and you
> shall call his name Jesus, for he will save his people from
> their sins." All this took place to fulfil what the Lord had
> spoken by the prophet: "Behold, a virgin shall conceive
> and bear a son, and his name shall be called Emmanuel"
> (which means "God with us"). When Joseph woke from
> sleep, he did as the angel of the Lord commanded him;
> he took his wife to his home; and he had not known her
> when she bore a son; and he called his name Jesus.

This translation follows the judgement of many patristic, medieval, and modern interpreters, according to
whom, even before the angel appears to him in a dream,
Joseph has learned about the virginal conception from
Mary. His reaction is one of reverence and religious fear
before the tremendous mystery: 'God is at work here.
I must leave.' His decision is not to divorce Mary but
to withdraw, gently and courteously, from the woman

who carries a child conceived through divine interven-
tion. The angel's message is not to inform him of the
virginal conception, as if he were ignorant of it, but to
reassure him that God does not want him to leave the
pregnant Virgin's side; instead he must take her to his
home and care for her and her child.[33]

Everything turns on the word translated by the Revised
Standard Version as 'to send away', which we have ren-
dered as 'to withdraw from': *apolysai*. The ordinary meaning of the Greek verb *apolyô* is 'to set free', 'to release on
receipt of a ransom' (hence *apolytrôsis*, 'ransom', 'redemption'). It can also mean 'to send away', hence 'to break
the bonds of marriage', hence (possibly) 'to divorce'. But
that cannot be its meaning here. How could Joseph 'divorce' Mary 'quietly', 'discreetly', 'in secret' (*lathra*)? Divorce, for Palestinian Judaism of the first century as for
late twentieth-century Britain, is a public act. Joseph's action (and its motives) must be quite different. Like the
other 'just men' of the Bible (Moses before the burning bush, Isaiah in the Temple, Peter after the miraculous shoal of fish), he feels fear before the All-Holy God.
When he considers that the 'Son of the Most High' has
been conceived as a human baby, through the overshadowing of the Holy Spirit, in the womb of a virgin, he
wants to depart, to leave the scene. This is the interpretation of St Bernard, derived, he says, from the Fathers.

> Joseph wanted to leave her for the same reason Peter
> begged the Lord to leave him, when he said, "Depart
> from me, O Lord, for I am a sinful man", and for the same
> reason the Centurion kept him from his house, "Lord, I
> am not worthy that thou shouldest come under my roof."

[33] De la Potterie, *Marie*, 87–97.

Thus Joseph, considering himself unworthy and a sinner, said to himself that a man like him ought not to live under the same roof with a woman so great and exalted, whose wonderful and superior dignity filled him with awe. He saw with fear and trembling that she bore the surest signs of the divine presence, and, since he could not fathom the mystery, he wanted to depart from her. Peter was frightened by the greatness of the power; the Centurion feared the majesty of the presence. Joseph, too, as a human being, was afraid of the newness of the great miracle, the profundity of the mystery, and so he decided to leave her quietly. Are you surprised that Joseph judged himself unworthy of the pregnant Virgin's company? After all, have you not heard that St Elizabeth, too, could not endure her presence without fear and awe? As she says, "Whence is this to me that the Mother of my Lord should come to me?" This then is why Joseph decided to leave her.[34]

St Thomas gives a similar reading: 'Joseph wanted to give the Virgin her freedom, not because he suspected her of adultery, but out of respect for holiness; he was afraid to go and live with her.'[35] The same opinion is held by the great theologian of the Council of Trent, Salmerón, and by numerous contemporary exegetes, including Canon Laurentin, Canon McHugh, and Father de la Potterie.[36] Perhaps the most poignant expression of St Joseph's holy

[34] *In Laudibus Virginis Matris, Sermo II* 14; *Sancti Bernardi Opera*, vol. 4, ed. J. Leclercq, O.S.B., and H. Rochais (Rome, 1966), 31f.

[35] ST Supplement 3a 62, 3, ad 2. Cf. *Scriptum super IV Librum Sententiarum* d. 30, q. 2, a. 2, ad 5.

[36] A. Salmerón, *Commentarii in Evangelia* 3 (Cologne, 1612), 237; R. Laurentin, *The Truth of Christmas*, 267f.; J. McHugh, *The Mother of Jesus in the New Testament* (London, 1975), 167ff.; de la Potterie, *Marie*, 93ff. In the patristic age, this interpretation can be found, among others, in Eusebius of Caesarea (*Quaestiones Evangelicae* 1, 3; PG 22, 884B–884D).

fear is in one of the hymns of St Romanos the Melodist (sixth century):

> Then Joseph, who never knew the Virgin, stopped,
> stunned by her glory,
> And, gazing on the brilliance of her form, said:
> 'O shining one, I see that a flame and hot coals encircle
> you.
> It frightens me, Mary. Protect me, do not consume me!
> Your spotless womb has suddenly become a fiery furnace.
> Let it not melt me, I beg you. Spare me.
> Do you wish me, like Moses of old, to take off my shoes,
> That I may draw nigh and listen to you, and taught by
> you say:
> Hail, Bride unbrided!'[37]

The relevance of this exegesis to our theme is as follows. *Like Elizabeth, Joseph sees the pregnant Mary as the greatest-ever shrine of God.* Like Moses, he wants to hide his face. He knows that he is standing on holy ground. He cannot endure the near presence of the fiery Godhead in the virginal bush. With the eyes of Isaiah, he sees God filling the temple of Mary's womb, and he cries, 'Woe is me! For I am lost . . .' (cf. Is 6:5). This reaction is particularly fitting in a man of the lineage of David and Solomon, the father who promised God a house in which to dwell and the son who had it built. Indeed, the exact prototype of Joseph's response is his forefather David's: 'How can the Ark of the Lord come to me?' (2 Sam 6:9). After all, the whole purpose of Matthew's narrative is to show that, despite the miracle of his virginal conception and the physical discontinuity in the genealogy (cf. Mt 1:16), Jesus is still of the Davidic line through his

---

[37] *Canticum in Annuntiatione* 15; SC 110, 36.

adoptive link with Joseph, hence the unusual wording of verse 18: 'The origin (*genesis*) of Jesus as Messiah'.

Joseph shows himself to be the purest of the sons of David: a just man who honours the Temple (Mary) and worships the God who dwells within it (Jesus). It is intrinsic to the logic of both infancy Gospels that his marriage to Mary be one of absolute virginal continence. Thus the humble man who does not dare approach the shrine becomes its guardian, the protector of the Virgin Theotokos and of her womb's divine burden. Like that of all the saints, Joseph's justice is one of radical obedience. The ever-greater God leads him beyond his own instincts of piety to a harder and yet infinitely more glorious holiness.

III

A WOMB WIDER THAN HEAVEN
THE TEACHING OF THE FATHERS

'The hearts of the Fathers', said Johann Adam Möhler (1796–1838), 'were full of Jesus Christ.'[1] They preferred nothing to the love of Christ, hence the power and undying youthfulness of their doctrine. In particular, the thought that God the Father's coeternal Word stooped to take upon him our embryonic human life and lived and grew in the womb as we do filled them with a love of astonished gratitude. This is one of the chief motifs in the dogmatic poetry of St Ephrem (c. 306–373), Syriac 'Harp of the Spirit'.

> It is a source of great amazement, my beloved,
> that someone should enquire into the wonder
> of how God came down
> and made his dwelling a womb,
> and how that Being
> put on the body of a man,
> spending nine months in a womb,
> not shrinking from such a home;
> and how a womb of flesh was able
> to carry flaming fire,
> and how a flame dwelt
> in a moist womb which did not get burnt up.
> Just as the bush on Horeb bore

[1] *Athanasius der Grosse und die Kirche seiner Zeit*, Zweites Buch (Mainz, 1827), 131.

God in the flame,
so did Mary bear Christ in her virginity.
Perfectly God,
he entered the womb through her ear;
in all purity the God-Man
came forth from the womb into creation.[2]

Much later, in the seventh century, when imperially
sponsored heresies were attacking the human freedom and
activity of Christ, St Sophronius of Jerusalem, champion
of christological orthodoxy, includes the nine months in
Mary in his synodical confession of faith. It is a broadside
against Docetism, indeed, against every attempt to deny
the reality or integrity of the manhood of God the Son.

The Word was truly made flesh and man from the undefiled and virginal blood of the all-holy and immaculate
Virgin Mary and was carried in the virginal womb and
completed the time of normal gestation, becoming like
us men in all natural things, though without sin, not dis-
daining our passible low estate. . . .[3]

When he preaches on the Annunciation, he lingers over
the same mystery:

She was pregnant with God . . ., with him who is glorified in heaven with the Father, but who on earth, in the
flesh taken from her, deigns to be carried in the womb.[4]

St Anastasius of Sinai (d. c. 700), who succeeded Sophronius and Maximus in the struggle against christological
heresy, observes that, if he had so desired, the omnipotent

---

[2] S. Brock, *The Harp of the Spirit: Eighteen Poems of St Ephrem* (London, 1983), 62f.

[3] *Epistola synodica*; PG 87B, 3162D.

[4] *Oratio II in SS. Deiparae Annuntiationem* 46; PG 87B, 327B.

Word could have bypassed human infancy altogether and created for himself an adult human nature.

> For he who had made Adam and brought him into being from non-being, without woman, womb, or birth, could have constructed an adult human nature for himself and dwelt in it and lived in this way in the world.[5]

But he did not. The Son of God emptied himself and accepted the whole slow development of human life from conception to the last breath. He condescended to be conceived and carried in the womb, to take flesh from, to be 'made from' (cf. Gal 4:4), a woman. A Victorian woman poet intuited the truth as swiftly as the Fathers:

> No sudden thing of glory and fear
> Was the Lord's coming; but the dear
> Slow Nature's days followed each other
> To form the Saviour from his Mother.[6]

When we say that the Word was made flesh, we mean that he humbled himself to become the Virgin Mary's tiny baby. By assuming human nature at his conception, God the Son made his own the frailness, the utter helplessness of life in the womb. St Jerome (c. 342–420) speaks with typical vigour:

> The Son of God, for our salvation, became Son of Man. He waits nine months to be born. He endures discomforts. Bloodied he comes forth. He is wrapped in swaddling clothes. He is covered in kisses.[7]

St Cyril uses the regular Greek word for 'fetus', when he says that it was not through sexual intercourse but by the

[5] *Viae Dux adversus Acephalos* 13, 8; CCSG 8, 243.

[6] Alice Meynell, 'Advent Meditation', *Poems* (London, 1914), 53.

[7] *Epistola XXII* 39; PL 22, 423. The word translated here as 'discomforts' (*fastidia*) is used by Virgil in the Fourth Eclogue (line 61).

Holy Spirit that the Holy Virgin became pregnant with the divine *brephos*.[8]

This is the scandal of the Incarnation. It was too much for the Manichees. According to Pope St Leo the Great (d. 461), they found the thought of the Logos being an unborn child particularly distasteful.

> It seems scandalous to them to believe that God, the Son of God, enclosed himself in a woman's innermost parts (*viscera*) and that his Majesty was submitted to the indignity of involvement with the nature of flesh and birth in the true body of human nature.[9]

The figure of the pregnant Theotokos was a sign of contradiction for those twin tendencies in antiquity—hatred of the body and contempt for women. The third-century Neoplatonist sage, Porphyry of Tyre, argued that it was absurd for Christians to accuse pagans of believing that their gods dwelled in idols of wood or stone. Even if this were true, their 'understanding would be much purer than that of a person who believes that the Divine entered the womb of the Virgin Mary, became a fetus, was born and wrapped in swaddling clothes, full of blood of the membrane, bile, and things much stranger than these'.[10] Whether or not their author was a renegade Christian, these supercilious remarks confirm St Augustine's judgement that Porphyry 'shied away from the saving humility' of God-made-man.[11] The Neoplatonist prides himself in his soul's capacity to escape the flesh and ascend to the One. The Christian God who, with-

[8] St Cyril of Alexandria, *In Joannis Evangelium* 5 [Jn 8:39]; PG 73, 876C.

[9] *In Epiphaniae Solemnitate Sermo IV* 4; SC 22B, 246.

[10] A. Harnack, *Porphyrius: Gegen die Christen* (Berlin, 1916), fr. 77.

[11] St Augustine, *De Civitate Dei* 10, 28; CCSL 47, 303f.

out ceasing to be God, descends into flesh and blood, into the womb of a virgin, arouses only his disgust.

The Fathers, by contrast, praise God the Son for his readiness to descend to the very sea-bed of our nature, to share our life's journey from its humble beginnings. As St Hilary (c. 315–367) says, 'the invisible Image of God did not scorn the shame that marks the beginnings of human life.'[12] 'When thou tookest upon thee to deliver man', sings the Church in the *Te Deum*, 'thou didst not abhor the Virgin's womb.'

The Theotokos as Sanctuary

Building on the testimony of the infancy Gospels, the Fathers apply the Old Testament images of God's presence to the Christ-carrying womb of the Virgin. It is the ultimate Temple, Tabernacle, the Palace of the Great King, the Ark of the Covenant, the Altar of Incense, the Throne of the Cherubim, the Sanctuary of God. Without loss of his divine immensity, in the smallness of his unborn humanity, God the Word is enshrined for nine months within Mary.

> Mary's womb filled me with wonder that it should contain you, my Lord, and enclose you.
> The whole of creation was too small to conceal your greatness,
> Earth and heaven too narrow to serve as embracing arms, to conceal your divinity.
> The womb of the earth is too small for you, and yet the womb of Mary is large enough for you.[13]

[12] St Hilary, *De Trinitate* 2, 24; CCSL 62, 60f.
[13] *Des heiligen Ephraem des Syrers Hymnen de Nativitate* (*Epiphania*) 23, 11; German translation by E. Beck, CSCO, *Scriptores Syri* (Louvain, 1959), 108.

In the Syriac school, St Ephrem has what one might call a 'locational' Christology. He sees the divine Word taking up a series of residences, each of which, in some sense or other, is a womb: the heavenly womb of the Father in which he is eternally begotten in his divinity, the earthly womb of the Blessed Virgin in which he is conceived and carried in his humanity, the watery womb of the Jordan in which as man he is baptized, the deathly womb of Sheol into which in his human soul he descends.

Something similar can be found in the tradition of Constantinople, in the homilies of St Proclus (d. 447), the defender of the divine motherhood. He regularly compares and contrasts the bosom of the Father and the womb of the Mother: 'Incarnate from the Virgin, he did not denude the Father's bosom; in heaven without mother God from God, on earth from a Mother the Lover of Men made man for men, sanctifying by his residence there the spotless womb.'[14]

According to the Fathers, God the Word treats Mary's womb with infinite courtesy and gentleness, leaving, as he enters, without breaking its maidenly seal. It is God's inviolable sanctuary, and, like the Temple in Jerusalem, says St Ambrose, its gate remains shut.

> What is this "gate of the sanctuary", this "outer gate towards the East" that remains closed, and "no one shall pass through it, except the God of Israel"? Is this gate not Mary, through whom the Redeemer entered into this world? This is the gate of justice. . . . This gate is Blessed Mary, of whom it is written that "the Lord will pass through it, and it shall be shut" after birth, because she conceived and gave birth as a virgin.[15]

[14] *Oratio V (De Laudibus S. Mariae)* 2; PG 65, 717C.
[15] St Ambrose, *Epistola* 42, 6; PL 16, 1126A. St Proclus says: 'He en-

As the most perfect sanctuary in revelation, the Immaculate Virgin's womb, like her heart, is consecrated for
ever to God, and to him alone. She conceives as a virgin,
she gives birth as a virgin, and remains for ever a virgin.
St Ambrose speaks for all Christendom when he asks:

> Would the Lord Jesus have chosen for his Mother a woman
> who would defile the heavenly chamber with the seed of
> a man, that is to say, someone incapable of preserving her
> virginal chastity intact?[16]

Mother of Manna

The cultic imagery applied by the Fathers to the pregnant
Theotokos eventually becomes eucharistic. 'Mary', says
St Ephrem, 'gave us the living bread instead of the bread
of trouble, which Eve gave.'[17] She carries in her womb
him who is the Bread of Life, the heavenly Manna.[18]
Since, from the first moment of the Incarnation, the attitude of Christ is one of self-offering, the virginal womb
can be hailed by St Andrew of Crete (c. 660–674) as the
'altar on which Christ the Lamb is mystically offered up

---

tered without passion. He left without corruption, as Ezekiel says . . .'
(*Oratio I* [*De Laudibus S. Mariae*] 1; PG 65, 692A).

[16] St Ambrose, *De Institutione Virginis* 6, 44; PL 16, 317. In the thinking of the Fathers, there is a regular correspondence between the virginal womb and the empty tomb. To take one of countless examples, St
Augustine says: 'The flesh in which he was born, coming out through
the closed womb as little, is the flesh in which he was resurrected, going
through closed doors as great' (*Sermo* 215; PL 38, 1074). The Church's
teaching on Our Lady's virginity *in partu* was powerfully reaffirmed
by Pope John Paul II in Capua in 1992 (*L'Osservatore romano*, June 10,
1992, 13ff.).

[17] *De Azymis* 6, 7; ed. T. J. Lamy, 1:593.

[18] St Proclus, *Oratio VI (De Laudibus S. Mariae)* 17; PG 65, 756A.

as a living, whole burnt-offering'. She is the table 'upon which Christ the heavenly bread, the Lamb offered up for all, is immolated as oblation and living victim'.[19] According to St Ambrose, there is an analogy between the wonderful change of bread and wine into the Body and Blood of Christ and the miracle of the virginal conception and birth.

> It is clear that the Virgin gave birth outside the order of nature, and what we confect is the body from the Virgin. Why, then, do you look for the order of nature in the Body of Christ, when the Lord Jesus himself was born of the Virgin outside of nature?[20]

Medieval and modern descriptions of Mary as ciborium and monstrance will only be elaborations of these patristic intuitions.[21]

Nestorianism and the Unborn Christ

Christ's presence in his Mother's womb was for four centuries an object of quiet contemplation. In the fifth century, it became a matter of loud contention. The Christology of Nestorius (d. c. 451), despite his insistence that he taught 'one Christ, one Son, one Lord', threatened to divide the incarnate Lord into two separate persons. It is a theory of inhabitation: the man Jesus is the temple in which the divine Word dwells.[22] God the Word 'attached' or 'conjoined' himself to a man and

[19] *Oratio IV in Nativitatem B. Mariae*; PG 97, 880A–880B.
[20] *De Mysteriis* 53; FC 3, 248.
[21] See N. Garcia Garces, 'La Virgen y la Eucaristia en la himnografia medieval', *Ephemerides Mariologicae* 2 (1952), 205–45, passim.
[22] F. Loofs, *Nestoriana: Die Fragmente des Nestorius* (Halle, 1905), 166, line 26; 168, line 3; 175, line 1; 242, lines 16 and 17; 278, line 3.

dwelt inside him.[23] Mary may not, therefore, be called
'Theotokos'. She gave birth to a man who was the residence or instrument of the Godhead but not himself God.
We cannot say that God became a child (*brephos*, unborn
or born) but only that he was the inhabitant of a child.

St Cyril of Alexandria regarded this theology as the
overthrow of the Incarnation. God the Word, he said,
did not come to lodge in a man; no, without ceasing to
be God, he truly became a man; he took flesh animated
by a rational soul and made it his very own.[24] It is not
enough to say that God is *in* this Child Jesus. This Child
Jesus *is* God, God the Word made true and perfect man.
We worship, not a divinized human, but a humanized
God.[25]

The language of indwelling is inadequate to describe
the union of divinity and humanity in Christ. St Cyril
was aware that Jesus called his body a temple (cf. Jn 2:21),
and that St Paul spoke of the Godhead deigning to dwell
bodily in Christ (Col 2:9; cf. 1:9). Consequently, even
in the central heat of the Nestorian controversy, he does
not discard the imagery of inhabitation. He applies the
Proverbs text—'Wisdom has built herself a house' (9:1)
—to the divine Wisdom's fashioning of a body for himself
in the Virgin's womb,[26] and so he can accept the assertion
in the Formula of Union that 'God the Word . . . from

[23] See St Cyril's account in *Adversus Nestorium* 1, 2; PG 76, 29A.
[24] Loofs, *Nestoriana*, 292, lines 1–6.
[25] *Adversus Nestorium* 1, 2; PG 76, 28D.
[26] *Thesaurus* 15; PG 75, 261C. In similar fashion, St Augustine says:
'The Wisdom of God, that is, the Word coeternal with the Father, in
the Virgin's womb built himself a house, a human body' (*De Civitate
Dei* 17, 20; CCSL 48, 588). In the Middle Ages, St Bernard sees Mary
herself as the house (*De diversis* 52, 2; PL 183, 674D). Earlier, Pope
St Leo the Great seems to have both ideas: 'In Mary and from her

the moment of conception united to himself the temple he had taken from [the holy Virgin].'[27] What matters to him is not so much the words a man uses as the meaning he gives them. It is not the Antiochene strangeness of Nestorius' vocabulary to which Cyril objects, it is the thinking that his vocabulary clothes. Nestorius' meaning is not the Church's. The dwelling of the Word in the temple of his body is not 'relational' (*schetikê*), like the divine indwelling that the just enjoy by grace, but unitive, realized by uniting humanity to himself hypostatically. The Son makes the animated body taken from the Virgin his *very own temple* (*idion . . . naon*).[28] In the words of St Athanasius, his predecessor in the see of Alexandria, 'in the Virgin [the divine Word] constructed for himself a temple, the body, and appropriated it as an instrument in which to dwell and be known.'[29]

St Cyril and St Proclus gradually realized that the temple and dwelling-place images of Scripture, indeed all the figures of containment and enclosure, apply with greater precision to the Mother of God than to her Son. The Lord Jesus Christ is Emmanuel, God-with-us, God-made-man, God the Word personally present in the flesh. When for nine months the Virgin carries him in her womb, she is the consummate Ark and Temple of God. In a homily preached at the Council of Ephesus, Cyril salutes Our Lady in a litany replete with the metaphors of habitation and sanctuary:

"Wisdom built himself a house"' (*In Nativitate Domini Sermo V* 2; SC 22B, 114).

[27] DS 272.

[28] *Quod unus est Christus*; SC 97, 294.

[29] *De Incarnatione* 8, 3; PG 25, 109C.

> Hail, Mary Theotokos, . . . imperishable temple, place of
> him who cannot be contained in a place, mother and vir-
> gin . . . , hail, thou who hast contained in thy holy virginal
> womb him who cannot be contained.[30]

Proclus acclaims the holy Theotokos as 'the unsullied
shell that contains the pearl of price', 'the sacred shrine
of sinlessness', 'the costly alabaster box of spikenard', 'the
ark gilt within and without'.[31] All the sacred places, in-
stitutions, and actions of Israel reach their fulfilment in
Mary's womb.

> O womb in which the charter of our freedom was com-
> posed! O belly in which the weapon for smiting the devil
> was fashioned. . . . O temple in which God became a
> priest. . . . O womb wider than heaven! O offspring, price
> of the world's redemption! . . . This is the tabernacle of
> witness, from which God, the real Jesus, after the nine
> months period as an embryo, came forth.[32]

St Cyril and St Proclus showed Nestorianism to be a
heresy that removes God as far as possible from the womb
and from birth, from the experience of having and being
in a mother, just as it also distances him from pain and
from death. By a sad irony, this theology, with its intention to guard the humanity of Christ, ends up as Docetic:
the infancy and sufferings of the flesh are real enough,
but they are not God the Son's very own. The Nestorian
Logos is as distant as any Gnostic redeemer from human
pain and childhood. Nestorius would admit that the Second Person of the Blessed Trinity was associated with

[30] *Homilia* 4; PG 77, 992B.
[31] *Oratio VI (De Laudibus S. Mariae)* 17; PG 65, 753B.
[32] *Oratio III (De Incarnatione Domini)* 3; PG 65, 708A; *Oratio VI (De Laudibus S. Mariae)* 17; PG 65, 750B.

Mary's child, intimately linked with him, but he would
not confess, indeed he strenuously denied, that this babe
was God. He failed to see the truth that enthralled Cyril's
every fibre: in the Holy Virgin's womb, God the Word,
without change to his immutable divinity, assumed our
humanity at the moment of conception and so made our
unborn human frailty his own.[33] If Cyril is vehement (as
his modern detractors insist), it is with the vehemence
of love: he will not tolerate Nestorius' insult to the God
who, for love of mankind, emptied himself in Mary's
womb and took the form of a servant.[34]

Womb and Bridal Chamber

He hath set his tabernacle in the sun: and he, as a Bridegroom coming out of his bride chamber, hath rejoiced as
a giant to run the way (Ps 18:6; revised Douai version).

In the patristic vision, the Virgin's womb is not only
a church, the shrine of divine presence, it is also a chamber, the scene of divine nuptials. 'The nuptial union is
between the Word and the flesh', says St Augustine (354–
430), 'and the bridal chamber of the union is the Virgin's
womb.'[35] A century earlier, St Methodius of Olympus
(d. c. 311) applied to Christ's flesh the bridal titles in the

[33] According to Cyril, the Antiochene theologian Diodore of Tarsus
delayed the union of the divine Word with the man Jesus to the moment of birth (*Fragmenta Dogmatica* 17; PG 76, 1449D–1450A).

[34] In his *Apologeticus contra Theodoretum pro XII Capitibus*, St Cyril says:
'When the inglorious burden of the self-emptying dawns on you, marvel more vehemently at the love of the Son for us' (PG 76, 441B).

[35] *Enarrationes in Psalmos* 44, 3; CCSL 38, 495. St Augustine also says
that 'the Child-Bridegroom came forth from his chamber, that is, the
virginal womb, with his Mother's virginity unharmed' (*Sermo* 191, 1, 2;
PL 38, 1010).

Song of Songs (cf. Song 6:9).[36] As a consequence of the Nestorian controversy, this imagery, beautiful though it is, was felt by the Fathers to be ambiguous: the poetic personification of the flesh as 'bride' could be misunderstood as implying a duality of subjects in Christ. The chief adversaries of Nestorius—Cyril and Proclus—did not feel this embarrassment themselves and continued to apply Psalm 18:6 to the womb of the Theotokos.[37] For them, the 'bridal' flesh was not simply the individual human nature assumed by the Word but the whole of created flesh: when he becomes man in his Mother's womb, the Son of God becomes Head and Husband of all mankind, embraces us all with a spousal love. After Ephesus the corporate interpretation will become dominant, as can be seen in one of St Gregory the Great's *Homilies on the Gospels* (dating from the 590s).

> God the Father prepared the nuptials for God the Son when he united the Son to human nature in the Virgin's womb, when he wished him who was God before all ages to become man at a later age of the world. But though such a union ordinarily requires two persons, be it far from our thoughts to suppose that the person of God and our human redeemer, Jesus Christ, is made up of two persons. We do indeed affirm that he is made up of two natures and exists in two natures, but the belief that he is composed of two persons we avoid as heresy. Hence, speaking more plainly and safely, we may say that the Father arranged the marriage of his kingly Son by joining to him Holy Church through the Incarnation.[38]

[36] *Convivium Decem Virginum*, 8; PG 18, 136A.

[37] Cf. St Proclus, *Oratio I (De Laudibus S. Mariae)*; PG 65, 681A.

[38] *Homiliarum in Evangelia Liber II, Homilia* 38, 3; PL 76, 1283A–1283B. Cf. M.J. Scheeben, *The Mysteries of Christianity*, Eng. trans. (St Louis and London, 1946), 373.

The description of the virginal womb as Christ's 'bridal chamber' is liable to misunderstanding in another way. It does not sufficiently show that the Incarnation takes place through the Blessed Virgin's faith as well as in her flesh. She is not simply the scene of the Word's marriage to humanity, the impersonal place in which the knot of the two natures is tied. She is actively engaged, personally involved. God does not force his Son upon mankind. He wants humanity to welcome him. He wants the race to give the Word its nature freely, with a wifely love. Incarnation is not invasion. Thus, at the Annunciation Mary gives assent for us all. To paraphrase Chesterton, men are men, but at the great moment of the Incarnation, man is a woman, the Blessed Virgin Mary.[39] She says Yes to God as representative of humanity, indeed of all creation, and as such she is the Word's Bride. Mary is all at once, as St Ephrem says, Christ's Mother, Daughter, Sister, Handmaid, and Bride.[40]

The Ark's Final Transfer

When the Church begins to celebrate the falling asleep of the Mother of God, the Fathers make a direct connection between the womb that housed God and the tomb that could not hold his Mother. The reason for the bodily Assumption of Our Lady is her divine motherhood. 'It is in recognizing this Virgin as Mother of God that we celebrate her Dormition.'[41] For St John Damascene (c. 675–749), this is more than an argument of 'conve-

[39] G. K. Chesterton, *The Napoleon of Notting Hill*, new ed. (London, 1928), 14.
[40] *Hymnen de Nativitate* (see above, note 13) 16, 9–11, 76.
[41] *Homilia II in Dormitionem B. V. Mariae* 15; SC 80, 162.

nience' or 'fittingness'. There is a certain necessity about the glorification of the body that once contained God.

> It was necessary (*edei*) that she who had given hospitality to the divine Word in her womb should come to dwell in the tabernacles of her Son. . . . It was necessary that she who carried her Creator as an unborn child (*hôs brephos*) in her womb should live in the divine tabernacles.[42]

The Word was made flesh from Mary. His body was fashioned by the Holy Spirit out of her flesh and blood. Through his virginal conception, God the Son is 'one body' (*syssômos*) with his Mother; indeed, for nine months, like every other baby, his body is literally within hers. It is only right, therefore, that she should be 'one body' with him in glory. This is the conclusion of a sermon attributed to St Modestus of Jerusalem (d. 634).

> Because Mary was the Mother of the Giver of Life and Immortality, Christ our God and Saviour, Mary was made alive by him, so that she might be one body with him in incorruptibility for eternity. It is he who has raised her from the tomb and placed her beside him in a manner known only to him.[43]

All the Byzantine preachers return to this argument. Mary gave flesh and human life to him who is divine life and resurrection; she, therefore, now receives from him, in body as well as soul, a share in his own resurrected life. He who taught men to honour their fathers and mothers could not let his Mother, from whom he took his flesh, see dissolution in the tomb.[44] The Assumption is an application of the Lord's teaching when he raised Lazarus:

[42] Ibid., 14; 158.
[43] *Encomium in B. Virginem* 14; PG 86, 3312B.
[44] *Homilia I in Dormitionem B. V. Mariae* 4; 90.

'I am the resurrection and the life; he who believes in me, though he die, yet shall he live, and whoever lives and believes in me shall never die' (Jn 11:25f.). No one lives more truly in Jesus than Mary: he is flesh of her flesh. No one believes in him with greater devotion: 'Blessed is she who believed' (Lk 1:45). Thus the Theotokos is not detained by death and passes into glory.

One golden link above all dazzles the minds of the Fathers: the connection between Our Lady's virginity and her bodily glorification. Long before the first homilies on the Dormition, St Gregory of Nyssa (c. 330–c. 395) said that Mary's virginity was like a rock upon which death is dashed.[45] As Ever-Virgin Mother, Mary reveals that with God all things are possible. The world is not a closed system of corruption. When he is born of a Virgin and rises from the dead in the flesh, the divine Word breaks the cycle of Adam's decay. He comes to make all things new, to halt the decline into dust. How could he abandon the body in which his work of rejuvenation began?

> It was necessary [says Damascene] that she who in giving birth had preserved her virginity intact should keep her body without corruption, even after death.[46]

In the Byzantine sermons on the Assumption, all the Old Testament types of the God-bearing Mary are once more displayed: she is royal throne, spiritual Eden, burning bush. Her falling asleep, the Apostles' carrying of her body to the tomb, and then its entry into glory are the final 'transfer of the Ark'.

[45] *De Virginitate; Gregorii Nysseni Opera*, vol. 8/1, ed. J. P. Cavarnos (Leiden, 1952), 305f.
[46] *Homilia II in Dormitionem B. V. Mariae* 14; 158.

When King Solomon brought the Ark to rest in the temple of the Lord, which he himself had bought, he summoned "all the elders of Israel to Zion to bring up the Ark of the Covenant of the Lord out of the city of David, which is Zion". . . . Similarly, now, to bring to rest the spiritual Ark, not of the covenant of the Lord, but of the very person of God the Word, the New Solomon himself, the Prince of Peace and Master Maker of the Universe, has today assembled the hypercosmic orders of the heavenly spirits and the leaders of the new covenant: the Apostles with the whole people of the saints in Jerusalem. Through the angels, he takes the soul into the holy of holies, the true and heavenly archetypes, on the wings of the four beasts, and places it beside his own throne, inside the veil, where Christ himself has entered and gone before us in the body. As for [the Holy Virgin's] body, it is carried in procession, while the King of Kings covers it with the radiance of his invisible divinity, and the whole assembly of the saints walks before him with sacred acclamations and offering a "sacrifice of praise". And then the body is taken into the tomb as into a bridal chamber and, through the tomb, into the delights of Eden and the tabernacles of heaven.[47]

God's home has come home.

Ten Long Lunar Months

The reverence shown in these texts for the unborn child, for the human body, and for womanhood is without pagan parallel. Only in one place is there a kind of remote preparation: Virgil's Fourth Eclogue, which haunted the Fathers and the Middle Ages. The Emperor Constantine read it out at the opening of the Council of Nicaea.[48]

[47] Ibid., 12; 152f.
[48] *Oratio ad Sanctorum Coetum* 21; PL 8, 464B.

There are many resemblances to Isaiah and the Gospels. The poem speaks of a child 'whose birth will end the iron race at last and raise a golden through the world'. The world is beginning anew, the Virgin is returning, and the Serpent is to perish. These coincidences are remarkable enough, but most astonishing of all is that the poet appears to be addressing the child on the eve of his birth, or just after. He invites him to show gratitude for all that his mother has done for him through ten long (lunar) months. In a culture in which the unborn child was not regarded as a fully human being, in a world where abortion and infanticide were widely accepted, this attitude to pregnancy and infancy is unprecedented. The poet appears to be saying that glory is the gift of a *parvus puer*, a little, still-to-be-born boy. It is not surprising, therefore, that, four hundred years after his death, Virgil should have inspired the greatest of the Christian Latin poets. Only the Son in the Virgin's womb, says Prudentius (348– c. 410), can bring the world its golden age.

> O noble Virgin, do you see,
> As weary months of waiting end,
> that your unblemished purity
> Shines more lovely in motherhood?
>
> O what great joys for the world,
> Your chaste womb within it holds,
> Whence comes forth the golden age
> Whose light renews the face of earth.[49]

[49] *Hymnus VIII Kalendas Januarias*, lines 54–60; PL 59, 894A–895A. On the influence of Virgil's Fourth Eclogue, see A. Mahoney, *Vergil in the Works of Prudentius* (Washington, 1934), 144–47.

IV

PERFECTION FROM CONCEPTION
THE MIDDLE AGES

The medieval carol puts religion into song and dance.
Doctrine takes on a vernacular voice; the hymn becomes
a ballad. Some carols are dramatic in form—dialogues,
soliloquies, almost miniature mystery plays. The actors
on the stage of Christian revelation disclose thoughts
and feelings of which Scripture says little but which the
Church knows by the insight of faithful and loving meditation. One fifteenth-century caroller imagines the emo-
tions of the expectant Mother of God.

> Gracyusly
> Conceyuyd have I
>   The Son of God so swete;
> Hys gracyous wyll
> I put me tyll,
>   As moder hym to kepe.
>
> Withowt dystresse
> In grete lyghtnesse
>   I am both nyght and day;
> This heuenly fod
> In hys chyldhod
>   Schal dayly with me play.[1]

[1] R. L. Greene, *The Early English Carols*, 2d ed. (Oxford, 1977), 164f.
This is of particular interest because of the secular lyric upon which it is
consciously modelled: 'The prototype is a song of the genre in which

This carol is just one example of the medieval Christian's respectful fascination with the life of Jesus in his Mother's womb. The attitude is typified, in images of the Visitation, by Elizabeth's gesture of courtesy, gently laying her hand on her cousin, the shrine that holds her Lord.[2]

The Cistercians

The new religious foundations of the Middle Ages—first the Cistercians, later the Franciscans—excelled in devotion to the humanity of Christ and to the mysteries of his life on earth, not least its very first months. The greatest of the early Cistercians, St Bernard of Clairvaux (1090–1153), takes up all the domiciliary imagery of the Fathers when he speaks of the Christ-containing Virgin. In soul as well as in body, she is the 'house' that the divine Wisdom built for himself. The Son 'has prepared his Mother by faith and good works to be a dwelling-place worthy of his majesty'. Her womb harbours the uncreated Wisdom whom first she had conceived 'in her spotlessly pure spirit'.[3]

In his second sermon 'In Praise of the Virgin Mother', commenting on Jeremiah's prophecy that 'a woman will compass a man (*femina circumdabit virum*)' (Jer 31:22), Bernard defines the sense in which the encircled unborn Child is a 'man'.

---

a betrayed maiden laments her pregnancy. . . . The blessed state of the Virgin and her rejoicing would have the effect of a striking contrast to hearers familiar with the type of song parodied' (408).

   [2] See p. 131 below.

   [3] *Sermo LII (De Sancta Maria)* 2; *Sancti Bernardi Opera*, vol. 6/1, ed. J. Leclercq, O.S.B., and H. Rochais (Rome, 1970), 275.

Even while he was still unborn, Jesus was a man, not in age, but in wisdom, in vigour of mind, not of body, in the maturity of his mental powers, not in the development of his members. For Jesus was not less wise, or rather I should say was not less Wisdom, at his conception than after his birth, when he was a little one than when he was full-grown. Whether he was lying hidden in the womb or wailing in the manger, whether as a growing lad questioning the doctors in the Temple or as a man of mature age teaching among the people, he was in truth equally full of the Holy Spirit.[4]

To some modern readers, St Bernard appears to appreciate insufficiently the place of development in Christ's human knowledge from conception to manhood. He interprets the 'advancing' of Jesus 'in wisdom and age' (cf. Lk 2:52) as a showing of what he has always had rather than a getting of something new.

It was not that anything was added to him that he did not have before, but that there seemed to be an addition whenever he willed it to be so.[5]

After the time of St Bernard, Catholic theologians became dissatisfied with this position. It could be taken as saying that the Word only appeared to have the mind of a child—a kind of cognitive Docetism, placing an incredibly adult head on infant shoulders. In fact, of course, St Bernard is not robbing Our Lord's human nature (and childhood) of any essential feature. He wants simply to emphasize that, from the first moment of conception, the manhood of the eternal Son never lacked the supernatural powers and blessings appropriate to his divine

---

[4] *In Laudibus Virginis Matris Homilia II* 9; *Opera* 4:27.
[5] Ibid., 10; 28.

person and necessary for his saving mission. Elsewhere St Bernard acknowledges that there was real progress in Christ's experimental knowledge: 'He became what he was already, he learned what he knew before, and he looked in our nature for "windows" and "lattices" (cf. Song 2:9) through which he could closely observe our wretchedness and woe.'[6]

If this monastic theology has a shortcoming, it is its failure to state explicitly what Scholastic theology will later explain: there can be growth at one level of Christ's human knowledge and an abiding fulness at another. In the next century, St Thomas Aquinas will confess that he himself 'advanced in wisdom' on the subject of Christ's 'advance in wisdom' and came eventually to attribute a real acquired (experimental) knowledge to Christ. (The passage is one of the very few in his writings in which the Angelic Doctor speaks in the first person singular.)[7]

Guerric (d. 1157), disciple of St Bernard and second abbot of Igny, applies the text about the 'shortened word' (Rom 9:18; cf. Is 10:23 in the Septuagint) to the incarnate Logos in the womb and in the manger.

> He wanted, so to speak, to abridge and diminish himself to the point where he reduced himself from his incomprehensible immensity to the narrowness of the womb, and he who contains the world allowed himself to be contained in a manger.[8]

By taking flesh at conception, by becoming an unborn child and being born in human helplessness in Bethlehem, the Son of God teaches us to be humble and childlike if

---

[6] *Sermo LVI in Cantica* 1; PL 183, 1047B.

[7] ST 3a 12, 2: . . . *et mihi aliquando visum est.*

[8] *De Nativitate Domini, Sermo* 5; SC 166, 228.

we want to enter the Kingdom.[9] Guerric speaks not only
of the Virgin's encompassing of the Word in her womb
but also of the hospitality she gives him in her heart. The
latter makes possible the former.

> If you consider the [physical] narrowness of her womb,
> it is indeed a confined space. But if you take account of
> the breadth of her heart, it is a vast throne, and it was this
> breadth of heart that made the womb capable of contain-
> ing such great majesty.[10]

Guerric applies Christ's words about Mary of Bethany
—'Mary has chosen the best part' (Lk 10:42)—to the
Blessed Virgin Mary. The transfer of text is reasonable
because 'the one welcomed the Lord under her roof, the
other into the bridal chamber of her womb.'[11]

The English Cistercian, John of Ford, born in Devon
in the mid-twelfth century, says that, from the first instant
of his conception in the Virgin's womb, the incarnate Son
is anointed by the Father with the Holy Spirit 'beyond
all measure', and from that overflowing fulness we, his
Church, have all received, grace upon grace.[12] A century
later, St Thomas Aquinas will teach the same doctrine.[13]
Already in the womb, Christ is Head of the Church. Indeed, according to John, the embryonic Christ is already
in a sense carrying his Cross, for at his conception he
takes a passible and mortal human nature, the frail flesh
in which he will suffer and die.

[9] Ibid., 3; 230.
[10] *In Annuntiatione B. Mariae, Sermo III* 5; SC 202, 158.
[11] *In Assumptione B. Mariae, Sermo IV* 1; SC 202, 458.
[12] *Super Extremam Partem Cantici Canticorum, Sermo XXI* 6–7; CCCM
17, 184.
[13] ST 3a 34, 2.

From the very moment the Word was made flesh, the Lord Jesus carried his Cross. From that moment he was truly a man of sorrows and acquainted with grief. We believe the evangelist signified this when he said that "the Word was made flesh". By "flesh" he meant the capacity of the flesh to suffer and to suffer with. For what in all creation is more fragile than flesh, more delicate than flesh? Fragility, therefore, corresponds to Passion, suffering; delicacy to Com-passion, suffering-with. From these two, as from two planks, Christ's Cross is constructed. For to suffer and to suffer with, as St Gregory says, is Christ's true Cross, namely, affliction of body and compassion of mind, provided such a cross is borne for Christ and following Christ. Christ carried this kind of cross from his entry into his Mother's womb. He endured the confines of the virginal womb.

John suggests that Christ's unborn human life was 'perhaps more burdensome for him than for other infants'. After all, unlike human persons, this divine person has entered into embryonic life knowingly and willingly, and he has done so for a salvific purpose. He wants to find Adam and renew his nature from its tarnished beginnings.

The sense of pain could not be lacking in the One who had come to experience pain from his very beginnings and was as full of grace as he was full of knowledge and truth. And so even there "he bore our infirmities and carried our sorrows" (Is 53:4). In fact, he bore them all the more truly because knowingly and willingly which other infants go through in a kind of sleep of ignorance. There, in the confines of the womb, he sought and found the Adam he once had sought and not found when once he hid himself in Paradise. [In the womb] he extracted with his own hands the sting of sin that the serpent had inflicted on the first man. He accomplished his work and, even at this time, "wrought salvation in the midst of the earth" (cf. Ps 73:12). He busily and briskly purged human conception from uncleanness. Yes, [in his Mother's womb,] the Lamb of God was already taking away the sin of the world, doing penance for our crimes, enduring the weariness of nine months and constantly interceding for us to the Father.[14]

To understand this passage correctly, we must recall that the 'knowingly' and 'willingly' here refer not only to Christ's divine knowledge and will (the one divine knowledge of Father, Son, and Spirit), by which the assumption of human nature at conception was eternally planned, but also to his human intellect and will. The difficulties of attributing such perfections to an unborn child will be considered below.

The Franciscans

Devotion to the infancy of Christ, including his first nine months of life, is one of the pillars of Franciscan spirituality. St Francis of Assisi (1181–1226) could not say the word 'Bethlehem' without bleating like a sheep, so overcome was he by knowing that the Creator of the universe had for sinful mankind's sake become a *puer pauperculus*, 'a poor little boy'.[15] It is not surprising to discover, therefore, that the feast of the Visitation of Our Lady was first celebrated by the Friars Minor, apparently on the advice of St Bonaventure, before being extended

[14] *Super Extremam Partem Cantici Canticorum, Sermo LXXXIII* 2; CCCM 18, 570. On the virginal conception and original sin, see *Sermo VIII* 4; 17, 81f.

[15] Thomas of Celano, *Vita Prima* 86.

to the whole Church in 1389 in the hope that Christ
and his Mother would visit the Church anew to put an
end to the Great Schism.[16] The link with Bonaventure
is of interest because of his own rich teaching on the
life of Jesus in Mary's womb. In his second sermon on
the Epiphany, he says that the first 'house' of the Child
Jesus, the house in which he was formed and found by
Joseph and the angels, was 'the house of the Virgin's
womb'.[17] He was first found in Nazareth in Mary as conceived, in Bethlehem with Mary as born, in Jerusalem by
Mary as adult. The Magi 'gave great honour to Christ
and his Mother, who conceived and carried him'.[18] In a
sermon on the epistle for the Purification of the Blessed
Virgin Mary (cf. Malachi 3:1), he finds the classical four
levels of meaning in the word 'Temple'. In its literal
meaning, it is 'the material basilica'; allegorically, the Virgin's womb; in its moral sense, 'the faithful soul'; in
its eschatological sense, 'the heavenly Jerusalem'. Of the
Virgin's womb, he says that it is a temple made by the
Father's power, adorned by the wisdom of the Son, dedicated by the grace of the Holy Spirit, filled by the presence of the Word made flesh, his 'special temple and
hospice'.[19]

St Thomas Aquinas

In the *Summa Theologiae*, St Thomas Aquinas devotes
four questions to the life of the unborn Jesus. Such at-

[16] See pp. 121ff. below.
[17] *Sermo II in Epiphania; Opera Omnia Sancti Bonaventurae* vol. 9
(Quaracchi, 1901), 151.
[18] *Sermo III in Epiphania*, 157.
[19] *De Purificatione BVM, Sermo IV*, 651.

tention would not have seemed excessive in the Middle
Ages.

> When we are speaking of God made man, these months
> in the womb are, theologically speaking, as precious as his
> birth and life upon earth. This may be unwonted in mod-
> ern theological thinking but came naturally to St Thomas
> and medievals generally. To be born of the Virgin Mary
> connotes a unique conjunction of the divine and the hu-
> man from the outset. This is the truth that lies at the back
> of this series of articles.[20]

I have shown already how the monastic theologians of
the twelfth century readily attributed the fulness of the
grace of the Holy Spirit to the soul of Christ from his
conception. St Thomas and the other Scholastic theologians of the thirteenth century continue this teaching.
Union with the divine Word bestows on Christ's soul an
abundance of sanctifying grace. Now since it is in one instant that Christ's body is conceived, his soul created and
infused into his body, and the complete human nature
united to the Word, it follows that his soul is filled with
grace from his conception.[21] The Word incarnate in Mary
is 'full of grace and truth', and 'from his fulness have we
all received, grace upon grace' (cf. Jn 1:14, 16). The embryonic Christ is holy, the holy of holies, and at the same
time he is hallowing; his grace is intended to overflow to
others. The personal grace by which Christ's soul is sanctified is really identical with the grace that makes him the
Head of the Church, sanctifying others.[22] From his con-

[20] Roland Potter, O.P., in *St Thomas Aquinas: Summa Theologiae* vol.
52 (3a 31–37) (London, 1972), 158.

[21] ST 3a 34, 1.

[22] Ibid., 8, 5.

ception, even in the womb, the soul of Christ the Head is full of the grace that he communicates to his members. The Holy Spirit will not be given to the Church until Jesus has been glorified (cf. Jn 7:39), but he dwells in the sacred humanity from the beginning, from the moment he fashions that humanity in the Blessed Virgin's womb.

Breathing new life into an idea that stretches back to St Athanasius and St John Damascene, St Thomas says that the humanity of Jesus was the efficacious 'instrument' of his divinity for the purpose of sanctifying man.[23] This means that his every human action and experience, from conception onwards, has the power to save and make holy. According to the Angelic Doctor, from the first moment of his virginal conception, Our Lord had the full use of his human free will and thus was able to merit our salvation. Moreover, from conception, at the peak of his human soul, he enjoyed the beatific vision of God.[24] Even as unborn child, Jesus looked on the Father's face, and in the Father he saw his members and loved them. In *Mystici Corporis*, Pope Pius XII put the doctrine into language that is both intellectually precise and affectively tender.

> The loving knowledge with which the divine Redeemer has pursued us from the first moment of his Incarnation surpasses all the powers of the human mind; for by means of the beatific vision, which he enjoyed from the time he was received into the womb of the Mother of God, he has for ever and continuously had present to him all the

[23] Ibid., 7, 1, ad 3; 8, 1, ad 1; 13, 3.
[24] Ibid., 34, 3 (merit), 4 (beatific vision). On meriting from conception, see also *Scriptum super III Librum Sententiarum* d. 18, q. 1, a. 3.

members of his Mystical Body and embraced them with his saving love.[25]

Some modern theologians have been embarrassed by this view of Christ's pre-natal perfections. It is widely reckoned to make his humanity, if not unreal, at least incredible. Psychology, it is argued, has shown that mental development is intrinsic to human life, so that a child already free, already in the bliss of man's final destiny, would hardly seem to count as a child. He would be a sad infant prodigy, robbed of his childhood.[26] As for the general Thomist doctrine of Christ's human knowledge, Hans Urs von Balthasar regards its interpretation of the Passion as 'incredible'.[27] Most modern orthodox Catholic Christology—for example, the recent theses of the International Theological Commission—tends not to speak of vision and simply affirms the filial character of Christ's self-knowledge, his 'mission-consciousness', his human awareness of being the eternal Son sent by the Father to save us. Pope John Paul II, though he continues to speak of Jesus' vision of the Father 'at the summit of his soul', has not explicitly identified this seeing with 'beatific knowledge'.[28]

Despite its many difficulties, St Thomas' doctrine of

[25] DS 3812.

[26] Cf. Balthasar, *Das Ganze im Fragment: Aspekte der Geschichtstheologie*, new ed. (Einsiedeln, 1990), 283f.

[27] *Theologik II: Wahrheit Gottes* (Einsiedeln, 1985), 261n.

[28] 'The Consciousness of Christ concerning Himself and his Mission', in *International Theological Commission: Texts and Documents 1969–1985* (San Francisco, 1989), 308. See Pope John Paul's Christological catechesis of November 30, 1988 (*Giovanni Paolo II: Io Credo in Gesu Cristo, morto, risorto, asceso al cielo* [Casale Monferrato, 1990], 54). Balthasar's view of Christ's 'mission-consciousness' is expounded in

Christ's 'perfections from conception' may have something to teach us. It may protect truths of which modern minds have grown oblivious. If we admit this possibility, we would be well advised to review the theory sympathetically—at least as a kind of 'thought experiment'—and attempt to integrate its insights with those of more recent theology. He who is the Church's 'Common Doctor' deserves one final hearing. That is what I shall try to give him.

To modern theology's criticisms, St Thomas might answer that, on his view, whatever graced the unborn Christ Child perfected, but did not destroy, his real unborn human childhood. He quotes St Leo the Great with approval: apart from the virginal manner of his conception and birth, the Child Jesus is 'in no way dissimilar to the generality of human infancy'.[29] True, because of his dependence on the obsolete embryology of antiquity, St Thomas is forced to make Christ's womb-life differ from other children's not only because his conception is virginal, but also because his body, unlike theirs, is fully formed from conception and therefore sufficiently organized to be informed by a rational soul. There is nonetheless no doubt that, for St Thomas, the incarnate Word in his childhood is real child, in mind as well as body. Like St Paul, like us all, when Jesus was a child, he spoke like a child, he thought like a child (cf. 1 Cor 13:11), he *was* a child. The store of knowledge 'infused' by the Holy Spirit into his 'possible' (receptive) intellect does not interfere with the normal process of growth in knowledge

Theodramatik: Die Personen des Spiels. Teil 2: Die Personen in Christus (Einsiedeln, 1978), 149–85.
    [29] ST 3a 29, 1, ad 3.

through the operation of his 'agent' intellect. The marvels of extraordinary 'beatific knowledge' at his soul's summit (*superior pars animae*) do not rob its lower slopes of their precious ordinariness. He is both 'pilgrim' and 'beholder'.[30] St Thomas' Christology does not lead to the ridiculous conclusion that, in his Mother's womb, the Holy Child 'was thinking about the theorems of hydrodynamics and the Battle of Hastings'.[31] He is not engaged in the adult business of thinking at all. He is doing something much more important: in the earthly paradise of his Mother's body, he is resting and seeing and loving and praising the Father.

The Child Jesus sees the Father in a childlike way. What he sees, the one whom he sees, is unchanging, but how he sees him, and how that seeing bears upon the rest of his human experience, will depend on the stage of life in which he finds himself.

Modern man, despite his self-conscious psychological sophistication, has often failed to see what the medievals much more readily grasped—the wonderful potentialities of childhood, the child's capacity to receive what God has to give. For all its apparent inconveniences, the Scholastic doctrine of the perfections of the Child Jesus does at least confirm the uniqueness of the new esteem for childhood made possible by the Incarnation. Father Walter Farrell, O.P., explains it beautifully:

The perfection of the Infant obviously has a deeper significance than fittingness to the Son of God and the Mother of God. Here is underlined a truth that marks the sharp

[30] Cf. ST 3a 15, 10; 3a 46, 8.
[31] Cf. E. L. Mascall, *Christ, the Christian and the Church* (London, 1946), 53.

difference between the pagan and the Christian world. For here is written, in capital letters of perfection, the truth that the Infant, helpless though it be, is the equal on human grounds of any adult; and this from the first instant of its life. Where justice and charity are the bases of human life, this truth is evident; where physical strength is the foundation of human living, what chance has the infant?[32]

Many educators and pastors have noted the extraordinary spiritual capacities of children. It should not surprise us. The child, the young human being, like every human being, is naturally religious. However tarnished and obscured, the indestructible icon of God is in the soul of every child from the first moment of its creation and infusion into the body. As we saw in the first chapter, once there is a human body, there is a human being, a rational creature who is *capax Dei*, capable of receiving the grace of communion with God. In baptism, the guilt of original sin is remitted, and the child is divinized by grace. Even though he is not yet conscious of the fact, he is now a member of Christ, a child of the Father and temple of the Holy Spirit, a partaker of the divine nature. His adult Christian vocation will only be to become what he is by his baptism, what he is already as a Christian child. St Thérèse of Lisieux understood this truth very clearly. Shortly before her death, she saw her end in her beginning, her beginning in her end. In the servant, as in the Master, there is a coincidence of crib and cross.

It seems to me that, when I was three, I judged things as I do now. At four I was, it seems, in the same dispositions in which I find myself now.[33]

---

[32] *A Companion to the Summa*, 4 (New York, 1949), 151.
[33] Manuscript A of the Autobiography, 4 and 11. See also Daniel-Ange,

And in 1895 she wrote thus of the child in the state of grace:

> In the heart of a tiny child, the Spirit is already at work. If my work had not been raised to God from its awakening, what would I have become?[34]

If such was the childhood of a fallen daughter of Eve, what kind of child will the divine Second Adam be? In every little one of the human family there are hidden spiritual depths to which modern western culture, so materialistic and mechanistic, so contra-life and contra-child, blinds the eyes of the mind. If God-made-man is perfect man, we should expect there to be capacities realized in his childhood that in us may remain mostly dormant. A baby, unborn or born, does not act rationally and freely in the way in which an adult does, and yet he has the aptitude to be free. Reason does not come into existence from nothing on a child's seventh birthday. In a striking image, St Augustine says that in the infant (he is thinking of the unborn as well as of the born) reason is like a 'slumbering spark', waiting to be gradually awakened and enkindled by age.[35] A baby's knowing and wanting, however basic, are still acts of a human person, someone made in the image of God. They may not yet be functionally rational or free, yet metaphysically they are superior to the highest acts of a non-rational animal.

We might therefore interpret St Thomas as follows. *Through the perfecting of spiritual capacities to be found in ev-*

Ton enfant, il crie la vérité: Catéchisme pour théologiens (Fayard, 1983), especially 19f.

[34] A 40.

[35] *Epistola CLXXXVII* 8, 26; PL 33, 841.

ery unborn child, in the very poverty of His embryonic
humanity, the Redeemer in the womb is in some mysterious fashion able to know and say Yes to the Father.
'When Christ came into the world, he said . . . "Lo, I
have come to do thy will, O God"' (Heb 10:5f.). And
in seeing and obeying the Father, he sees us and enfolds
us in his love.

Our Lord's enjoyment of the beatific vision is not incompatible with genuine, complete, and credible childhood. The vision of God is, after all, a divine gift, not
a human achievement. It requires for its possession, not
maturity of mind or body, but simply the natural receptivity of the spiritual soul, its 'capacity for God'. Every
unborn child, made in the image of God, is capable of
being graced into communion with him. (This is the pre-
supposition of the Church's law, which provides for the
baptism of aborted fetuses, if they are alive, without re-
striction on age [cf. CIC 871]). If every child from conception is capable of relationship with God, it is surely
not unreasonable to hold that the eternal Son made man,
even in his Mother's womb, was bathed in the sunlight of
the Father's presence. As St Thomas teaches, in the very
instant of his conception, the soul of Jesus was created
and united to the Word in person, and so received more
fully than any other creature 'the influence of that light
in which God is seen by the Word'.[36]

The knowledge of the blessed is intuitive, not dis-
cursive, a contemplation, not a conclusion. It is not
at the front of Jesus' mind, but, as Jacques Maritain
suggested, is above consciousness and can therefore co-
exist with the slumbering semi-consciousness of the in-

[36] ST 3a 10, 4.

fant.[37] One might even say that, given childhood's natural receptivity and openness, there is something beautifully suitable about the Child Jesus, even as unborn, gazing on the face of the Father. Ferdinand Ulrich has argued that the child is 'contemplative', 'theoretical', in his very being, in his dependency, 'in the simplicity of his perception, the poverty of his openness, the unaffectedness with which he abandons himself to the other person'.[38] No one is more dependent, none more open or unaffected, than the unborn child, and so no one is more contemplative. The beatific knowledge of Christ could therefore be seen as working in and through this strictly objective 'contemplativeness' of unborn childhood.

Finally, in fairness to St Thomas, we must admit that his Christology does do justice to the Scriptural data concerning the human knowledge of Jesus. A threefold pattern emerges from a reading of the Gospels: an experimental knowledge in which Our Lord grows and develops (cf. Lk 2:52); an extraordinary prophetic knowledge of the future and of men's hearts (cf. Mt 9:4; 12:25 etc.); and an intimate knowledge of the Father that is higher and more direct than faith (cf. Mt 11:27ff.): St John's Gospel describes it as 'seeing' (cf. Jn 3:11; 31–32; 6:45f.; 8:38). Nowhere does the New Testament suggest that Jesus came to know that he was God the Father's eternal Son by deduction or by information from a human person. At no point does it describe him as a believer. He *just knows* the One who sent him and thus who he himself is and why he has come. This knowledge precedes and

[37] Cf. *On the Grace and Humanity of Jesus*, Eng. trans. (London, 1969), 48ff.

[38] *Der Mensch als Anfang: Zur philosophischen Anthropologie der Kindheit* (Einsiedeln, 1970), 146.

underlies all his other human knowing and is the source of his teaching's unique power. It is, says St Thomas, beatific knowledge and is enjoyed by Christ, in virtue of the hypostatic union, from the beginning, from conception.

The Carmelite theologian, Father François-Marie Léthel, who teaches at the Theresianum in Rome, has recently argued powerfully for St Thomas' doctrine of Christ's 'perfection from conception'.

> The affirmation of the human freedom of Jesus from the first moment of conception is without doubt unthinkable from the psychological point of view, but it is necessary from the christological point of view, and it necessarily implies vision. It is one of those extreme statements of St Thomas, a statement taken as far as it will go, a statement that people nowadays are tempted to reject, because they do not see its profound meaning. In fact, this extreme point in St Thomas' Christology is one of its most enlightening. It gives supreme value to the human freedom of the Son of God, which is as important as the grace of the Holy Spirit and is always linked with the grace of the Holy Spirit. The sacred humanity was never for one instant without grace or freedom. . . . This contemplation of St Thomas' gives new value and meaning to the whole earthly life of Jesus in its every moment, even the most hidden, even the most secret, such as the moment of his conception. Each of these moments has an infinite value for our salvation. . . . [F]rom the first moment of his conception, and at every moment of his life on earth, Jesus loves his Father perfectly, he glorifies him by his obedience, and at the same time he loves his whole Mystical Body, that is to say, the whole of the human race, which he has come to save, and each personally as if he were the only one. Because he first loved us in all his

earthly life, we can in return share in his whole earthly life. Nothing in it eludes us. The architecture of the merit of Christ guarantees, defends, and protects the space of total communion with Jesus: "*Jésus nous appartient tout entier*" (Péguy), "All Jesus is ours."[39]

Mother of the Eucharist

As we have already seen, the Fathers applied eucharistic imagery to the Mother of God. This is continued in the Middle Ages. We shall single out four texts. First, it is constantly emphasized that the Body received in Communion is none other than the true body born of the Virgin Mary, the body taken from her flesh and in her womb. St Peter Damian (1007–1072) says:

> The same body of Christ that the most blessed Virgin brought forth, which she nourished in her womb, wrapped in swaddling clothes and brought up with motherly care: this same body, I say, and none other, we now perceive without any doubt on the sacred altar.[40]

Two centuries earlier, St Paschasius Radbertus (c. 790–865), in his book *On the Body and Blood of the Lord*, compares the work of the Holy Spirit at the altar of the Church with his operation in the womb of the Virgin.

> If you believe that flesh to have been created from the Virgin Mary in the womb without seed by the power of the Holy Spirit, so that the Word became flesh, truly believe that this body taken from the Virgin is confected

[39] *Connaître l'amour du Christ qui surpasse toute connaissance: La théologie des saints* (Venasque, 1989), 293f.
[40] *Sermo XLV (In Nativitate BVM)*; PL 144, 743B.

[in the Eucharist] by the word of Christ and through the Holy Spirit.[41]

The Spirit is never a Spirit of disincarnation. His mission is always to bring us the flesh-and-blood reality of the Son of God. The realism of his eucharistic presence is a consequence of, and a kind of extension of, the Incarnation.

In his 'Letter to the Entire Order', St Francis of Assisi appeals for the utmost reverence, devotion, adoration, to be given to the Blessed Sacrament, especially by priests, and compares the Christ-carrying Virgin to the person who receives him in the Eucharist:

> If the Blessed Virgin is so honoured, as is right, since she carried him in her most holy womb . . ., how holy, just, and worthy must be the person who touches him with his hands, receives him in his heart and mouth, and offers him to others to be received.[42]

Finally, in one of the treatises in his commentary on the Magnificat, John Gerson (1363–1429), the great Chancellor of Paris, provides a Marian meditation on the Eucharist ('He has filled the hungry with good things'). He calls Mary 'Mother of the Eucharist' and asks for the help of her prayers when he receives Christ's Body and Blood.

> You, Mary, are Mother of the Eucharist, because you are Mother of Grace. . . . If, with your mercy and help, we receive your Son in the sacrament of the Eucharist, he will surely receive us and incorporate us into his Mystical Body.[43]

[41] *Liber de Corpore et Sanguine Domini* 4, 3: PL 120, 1279B–1279C.
[42] n. 21.
[43] *Tractatus IX super Magnificat, Opera Omnia,* 4 (Antwerp, 1706), 451.

This thought will be developed later in the French School.

A Worthy Dwelling for the Son

The final cause of the privileges of the Blessed Virgin Mary is her divine motherhood. As the Collect of the Immaculate Conception says, it was to make her a dwelling worthy of the Father's eternal Son that she was preserved from all stain of original sin from the first moment of her conception. Through the anticipated power of the Cross, the triune God engraced her at the beginning of her existence, so that she could be a fit sanctuary, in womb and in heart, for the coeternal Son. Most of the medieval theologians so far mentioned did not perceive this truth, but it was seen and proclaimed, to the glory of their order and homeland, by two British Franciscans—William of Ware and Duns Scotus.[44]

[44] The relevant texts from William of Ware and Duns Scotus are conveniently gathered in G. M. Roschini, *Mariologia*, new ed., 2 (Rome, 1948), 64–69.

V

FIRST STEP INTO THE WORLD
THE AGE OF BAROQUE

The Baroque is an age of paradox. Its paintings and buildings, its poetry and drama, above all its music, revel in
contrast and the coincidence of opposites. In the *Vespers*, Monteverdi wraps the luxuriance of his polyphony
around the plainness of the Church's chant. Don Quixote
is a wise fool. In the canvases of Rembrandt and La Tour,
light glows warmly in the dark. It should not surprise us,
therefore, to find the divines of the Baroque delighting in
the paradox of paradoxes—God almighty made helpless
unborn child.[1]

> This is, as it were, his first step, his entry into abasement
> and into the world. In this first step of the Son of God,
> at the start of his journey from heaven to earth, we have
> and we adore a speechless Infant-Word, an Infant-God, a
> God at once both mortal and immortal, a God suffering
> and impassible, a God eternal and measured by days and
> moments (which Nestorius could not understand), a God
> immense and enclosed within his Mother's womb.[2]

In the history of the Church, no school of theology
and spirituality has given Jesus' life in Mary more at-

[1] See the articles on 'Barock' in *Lexikon für Theologie und Kirche* 1,
1258–69.
[2] *Vie de Jésus* 25; Pierre Cardinal de Bérulle, *Oeuvres complètes*, new
ed. (Paris, 1856), 481. (Except where otherwise noted, all references
to Bérulle's works will be to this edition.)

tention than the seventeenth-century French School, of which Pierre Cardinal de Bérulle (1575–1629) was the founder.

A 'Copernican' Christology

The most marked feature of the theology of Bérulle is its Christ-centredness. Pope Urban VIII called him 'the Apostle of the Word incarnate', and one of his successors as Superior General of the French Oratory, Father Bourgoing, suggested that he had been sent by God 'as a new St John to point out Jesus Christ'.[3] To use one of his own favourite images, Bérulle worked a 'Copernican revolution' in the sacred sciences. He tried to do in theology what his older contemporary, Galileo, was doing in astronomy.

> One of the outstanding intellects of this age has tried to maintain that the sun, and not the earth, is at the centre of the universe. . . . This novel opinion, little followed in the science of the stars, is useful and must be followed in the science of salvation. For Jesus is the sun, immobile in his grandeur and moving all things. . . . Jesus is the true centre of the world, and the world must be in a continual movement towards him. Jesus is the sun of our souls, from whom they receive all graces, lights, and influences.[4]

For Bérulle and the other men and women of the post-Tridentine Church, even the lay-out of church buildings was an icon of Christ-centredness. The all-attracting focus for eye and thus for mind and heart was the tabernacle of the Presence at the centre of the high altar.[5]

[3] Preface, Oeuvres, 98.
[4] Grandeurs de Jésus 2, 2; 161.
[5] See J.-B. Thiers, Traité de l'exposition du Saint-sacrement de l'autel (Paris, 1673).

Bérulle's Christ-centredness is sound and Catholic. I say 'sound and Catholic' because it never makes the mistake of some later forms of christocentrism, which isolate Christ from either the Trinity or the Church. The God-Man, the incarnate Son, the centre of Catholic faith, is never separated from the Father and the Spirit, nor from the Virgin Mother and us his members. Bérulle's inspired insight is that the guarantee of an authentic Christ-centredness is Mary, above all the pregnant Mary. For nine months Jesus is quite literally in the centre of her body and the all-absorbing focus of her devoted love. If Jesus is the sun, Mary is the circling planet.

> He is a sun, and the Virgin is a planet that has its movements around Jesus, around this Sun of Glory. . . . He is her centre, and she is his circumference.[6]

The Lodgings of the Son of God

Like the Syriac theologians, Bérulle compares and links the diverse lodgings (*séjours*) of Jesus: the bosom of God the Father, the womb of the Blessed Virgin, the altar of the Catholic Church.

> There are three states of Jesus that deserve singular and daily consideration: in the womb (*sein*) of the Father as Son of God, God of God, consubstantial and equal with his Father; in the womb of the Virgin as Son of Man, both man and God, the Mediator of God and men; in the womb of the Church, which is his centre and altar, as Lamb of God and victim of praise and propitiation, which she [the Church] presents to the eternal Father.[7]

[6] *Vie de Jésus* 28; 494.
[7] *Opuscules de piété*, new ed. (Paris, 1943), chap. 38; 162.

Balthasar called Bérulle 'a great pray-er [*Beter*], more
specifically an adorer [*Anbeter*]'.[8] The marvel of the Incarnation is this: through it God worships God. God the
Son in his humanity adores God the Father, with whom,
in his divinity, he is coequal. What is more, this filial worship of the Father begins at the first moment of the Incarnation and has its first sanctuary in the Virgin's womb.
Bérulle, who had a thorough knowledge of the Greek
Fathers, repeats what Cyril and Proclus and Andrew of
Crete had recognized before him, namely, that the Virgin's pure womb, unshadowed by any sin, containing the
divine Word himself, is 'the holy or sacred temple where
Jesus reposes, the true Ark of the true Covenant . . . and
the Virgin's heart is the first altar on which Jesus offered
his heart, his body, his spirit, as a victim of perpetual
praise'.[9] When Christ comes into the world, he surren-
ders his new human body and will to the service of the
Father: 'Lo, I have come to do thy will, O God' (Heb
10:5ff.; cf. Ps 39:6–8). Bérulle follows St Thomas' teaching that, from the first moment of his conception, Christ
has the use of his human free will and at the summit of
his soul enjoys the beatific vision of God.

> He is living in the Virgin, and he is life itself. He is holy
> by the grace of the hypostatic union, which is the grace of
> graces. He is in glory by the state of his soul, established
> at the very hour of its making in the vision of God.[10]

Before he has the use of his senses, he enjoys the exercise
of his spirit. He cannot yet see bodies, but he can look at

[8] Introduction to Pierre de Bérulle, *Leben im Mysterium Jesu* (Einsiedeln, 1984), 13.
[9] *Vie de Jésus* 28; 494.
[10] Ibid. 24; 478.

the angels and the glory of heaven.[11] Jesus is in Mary 'as in a paradise where he sees God and enjoys his glory'.[12]

Even in the womb, Jesus is meriting our salvation and adoring his eternal Father, 'offering him his new life and his body destined to be host and victim for the human race'.[13] On entering into the world, he does not 'delay for a moment' to dedicate himself to the Father's will and thus to the Cross. From this first moment, we are 'engraved' into his heart and mind.[14]

The Unborn State of Christ

The Christology of Bérulle is a doctrine of *état*. This has many resonances, political as well as theological, in the language of seventeenth-century France. It signifies the 'divers estates' of mankind, the classes and orders of society, but even more importantly the conditions and stages of human life. Bérulle uses the concept of *état* to revive St Irenaeus' theology of recapitulation and the Thomist doctrine of Christ's headship.[15] As man, but because he is God, Christ is 'the head of human nature'.[16] In assuming a complete and concrete human nature, the universal Word in some way unites himself to every man, and, by living a complete human life from conception to the last breath, he touches and hallows every stage, every state, of every man's existence.

[11] Ibid.
[12] Ibid.; 479.
[13] *Opuscules de piété* 45; 185. Cf. *Vie de Jésus* 26; 486f.; 27, 491f.
[14] *Vie de Jésus* 30; 506.
[15] F. G. Preckler, *État chez le Cardinal de Bérulle: Théologie et spiritualité des états bérulliens* (Rome, 1974), 174 and passim.
[16] *Opuscules de piété* 45, 5; 185.

By this high, divine and lofty counsel, we do not just have
a Man-God, which is what the Incarnation gives us. We
have an infant God, a mortal God, suffering, trembling,
weeping in a cradle; a God living and walking on earth,
in Egypt, in Judaea. . . . God wants us to have all the mis-
eries, conditions, and lowlinesses of our nature relieved
by the divine subsistence and personality, a God suffering
and dying on the Cross, a God dead in the tomb, for he
who took our nature by the mystery of the Incarnation
wanted to take all these states and conditions of our nature
and to honour them with the divine subsistence, what the
ancient Fathers of the Church call the economy and dispensation of the divine mystery. For the Incarnation of
the Word is the basis and foundation of a supreme dignity,
in other words, not only of the sanctification but also of
the deification of all the states and mysteries that share
the life and wayfaring condition of the Son of God on
earth.[17]

The first state of the Word made flesh is infancy—
unborn infancy. 'The first way the Son of God chose to
honour his Father on earth is infancy, that is to say, abasement, subjection, and powerlessness'.[18] He could, had he
wished, have created an adult human nature for himself,
but that would have deprived his Mother and us of his
nine months in the womb. 'His love for her and for us
led him to be a child, both a child inside her and a child
outside her.'[19] He wanted not only to be a human being
but to be like other human beings in all things but sin.
This is for the purpose of a wonderful exchange: he is
like us in the infirmity of our nature, so that we can be

[17] Ibid., 46, 2; 187f.
[18] Ibid., 70, 3; 263.
[19] Ibid., 48, 4; 254.

like him in his grandeurs.[20] 'The Son of God, in clothing himself with our humanity, wanted to separate himself only from sin, not from infirmity.'[21]

His conception and life in the womb have a redeeming purpose. The virginal and miraculous character of his conception and his unique perfections as human child in the womb are intended 'to repair the ruins of our pitiful entry into the world as sinners'.[22] At our conception we contract, through descent from our father Adam, the guilt of original sin. The gateway of human existence needs rebuilding. Thus the eternal Son of the Father assumes human nature through a miraculous virginal conception and showers on unborn infancy a profusion of blessings. This places all natural conception and every unborn child in a new situation.

> Seeing that he wanted to be an infant on earth, in order to consecrate and sanctify human infancy contaminated by original sin, could this infancy have been better restored than by a virginal conception, a miraculous birth, a light of glory before the light of the world, a divine power in the powerlessness of the Child, the use of holy and perfect life with God his Father and the Virgin his Mother before the use of his senses and the force of nature?[23]

God-made-child sanctifies not only human life in the womb but all its properties. It is a state of total dependence of child on mother.

> But we see sensibly that in this present state she is more close and more conjoined, while he is in her, while he is

[20] Ibid.
[21] Ibid.; 256.
[22] *Vie de Jésus* 30; 505.
[23] Ibid.; 506.

part of her, while she lives for him, and he lives by her, and he is in a continual state of dependence and even of indigence with regard to her.[24]

Impuissance, incapacité, indigence: this is the condition of every unborn child, and this is the slavish condition, the *forma servi*, that the self-emptying Son of God has assumed for love of mankind. By this same path of voluntary vulnerability, he will go to the Cross. In obedience to the Father, loving mankind to the end, he will freely let himself be delivered into the hands of those who will kill him. The paradox is that this powerlessness, this 'deified incapacity', [25] has the power to conquer Satan. The way of weakness is a shining road, on which the royal banners forward go.

The Eucharist, like the womb and the Cross, is a mystery of power through powerlessness. Through the Spirit's work of transubstantiation, the Father's almighty Word incarnate places himself in the hands of priests.

He is all-powerful, but the All-Powerful comes to us through our wills and through our hands, as if he wanted to take up again on the throne of his power the same dependence he had in the state of his powerlessness, that is, in his infancy, as if he wanted to renew before our eyes the abasement he once took on earth.[26]

On earth under the sacramental species, as in his own species in heaven, the risen Lion of Judah is the slain Lamb of God.

---

[24] Ibid.; 493.
[25] *Opuscules de piété* 70, 3; 262.
[26] Ibid., 109, 2; 342.

The Visitation

The Visitation, says Bérulle, is the only visible work reported by Scripture that Jesus and Mary performed during the nine months the divine baby was in his Mother's womb.[27] It is 'the first operation of the Son of God made Son of Man, the first communication of Jesus and Mary in the universe', 'the first ray of the Sun of Justice'.[28] And who is the object of this visit from God incarnate and his Mother? 'Not Augustus, then triumphant in Rome, but a child hidden in his mother's womb in a village in Judaea'.[29] The little Baptist who does not yet know himself comes to know God and the Mother of God. Taking up a theme from the Fathers, Bérulle says that, in the womb of Mary, the Word is 'abridged': without change to his divine greatness, he takes on our human tininess.[30] These two marvels—God made man, and the Virgin made Mother—are not disclosed to the grandees of this world but to a little baby, 'because the order of Sacred Providence wanted to give the privilege to a child in honour of the divine childhood'.[31]

> God has become a child, and so he wants first to be known and adored by a child, and this is one of the first emanations of the childhood of God, manifesting himself to the universe. God is a child, the world ignores, heaven adores, and a child is the first person in the universe to recognize and adore him, and he does so by the homage and secret operation of God himself, who wants to act upon children. He wants to honour himself as child by

27 Ibid., 47, 4; 216.
28 Ibid., 47, 4–5; 217f.
29 Ibid., 47, 5; 218.
30 Ibid., 47, 6; 221.
31 Ibid.

giving the first knowledge of himself to a child in the
world, making him his prophet in the universe. Thus the
Infant-God is recognized and manifested, not by an angel,
but by a child. So his first prophet is a child, just as shortly
his first martyrs will be children.[32]

A child is 'the first disciple of the school and academy
of Jesus', 'the first officer of Jesus', the possessor of 'the
first state of his crown'.[33]

The Virgin fills this little child with joy and his mother
with the Holy Spirit, and the Virgin's tongue, more powerful than the tongues of fire that descended on the Apostles, fills the child and his mother with the fire of love
and the Holy Spirit, and she herself receives a new gift of
the Holy Spirit, a new elevation and a powerful rapture
that transports her into the lovely canticle of praise that
the Church has chosen for praising God every day of the
year.[34]

In the Incarnation, God takes the 'little way'. As a disciple
of Bérulle says, he who is great in the bosom of his Father
becomes small in his Mother's womb, 'the smallest of all
the children of men'.[35]

Jesus in Mary: A Union of Hearts

Between any expectant mother and the child in her womb,
there is more than a merely physical presence of the one
to the other, of the one in the other. The bodily closeness
is the basis of an intimacy of knowledge and love, a union

[32] Ibid.
[33] Ibid., 47, 7; 222.
[34] Ibid., 47, 3; 216.
[35] F. Bourgoing, *Méditations sur les divers estats de Jésus-Christ, Nostre
Seigneur* (Paris, 1648), 45.

of hearts. This natural bond is wonderfully strengthened
by the unique fulness of grace with which the God-Man
and his Mother, each in his own way, are endowed.

> These two hearts of Jesus and Mary, so close and con-
> joined by nature, are still more conjoined and intimate by
> grace, and they live the one in the other.[36]

Mary, full of grace, is totally centred on the Child-God
in her womb.

> All these senses are directed at him, for this is a sensible
> mystery, a mystery that is sensible in her. And the whole
> of human sensibility owes homage to its God made sen-
> sible for human nature. All her spirit is applied there. . . .
> The grace infused into the Virgin, grace so excellent and
> exalted, applies and absorbs all the senses, all the faculties,
> and all the spirit of the Virgin. . . . Thus grace and nature
> conspire in her to establish an excellent disposition, one
> that enraptures her heart and her soul in Jesus her Son and
> her God.[37]

'Great and happy sharings of Jesus with Mary!' Later
St Joseph and St John will have a part, but now, for nine
months, only the eternal Father and the Virgin Mother
share with Jesus.[38]

Bérulle's prose is perhaps not the most suitable instrument for expressing this great theology. Everything he
was trying to say is expressed much more tellingly by one
of his later compatriots—Paul Claudel, France's greatest poet of the last hundred years and an ardent devotee
of the culture of the Baroque. He beautifully describes

[36] *Vie de Jésus* 28; 494.
[37] Ibid.; 497.
[38] Ibid.; 495.

the heart-to-heart contact of the Virgin Mother with the Infant God within her:

> At the end of this third month after the Annunciation,
>   which is June,
> The woman who is God's has heard the tune
> Of heartbeats under hers and felt the movement of her
>   Son.
> Within the sinless Virgin's womb commences a new era.
> The Child who is before all time assumes time in his
>   Mother of his Mother,
> And in the primal Mover man's breathing is begun!
> She moves not, speaks not a word. She adores.
> She withdraws from the world. For her, God is not
>   outdoors:
> He is her work, her Son, her Baby, borne as her All!
>
> Satan rules and the whole wide world offers him incense
>   and gold.
> God penetrates like a thief in this Eden of death overbold.
> A woman was once deceived, and now a woman cheats
>   hell.
>
> O God, in a woman hid! O Cause, in this bondage bound!
> Jerusalem knows naught; even Joseph sees darkness
>   profound.
> The Mother alone with her Child feels his ineffable
>   moving.[39]

Mary's adoration of God incarnate within her, like her consent at the Annunciation, is representative; it is offered on behalf of the whole human race. For nine months, says Bérulle, Mary is the only person on earth who worships the mystery of the Incarnation. It takes place 'on the earth,

[39] Paul Claudel, *Coronal*. French text with Eng. trans. by Sister Mary David, S.S.N.D., (New York, 1943), 86ff.

for the earth, and yet is not known by the earth'. For the
benefit of the whole earth, Mary alone worships Jesus.[40]

Having housed the Son of God for nine months, in
Bethlehem Our Lady gives him to the world. This is her
everlasting mission. For ever in heaven as once on earth,
Mary has the power to give her Son to men. 'May she
use her power,' prays Bérulle, 'may she give him to us
and us to him.'[41]

The unique joint working of the Mother of God and
her Son, of Jesus with Mary and Mary with Jesus, is
prepared in advance by the Immaculate Conception. To
make her ready to be an earthly paradise for God the
Son, the Blessed Virgin is 'conceived without sin, sanctified from the first moment of her existence'.[42] Earth was
not worthy to receive him, but he chose for himself 'an
earth on the earth', which can take him in with unfalter-
ing and spotless faith.

> He happily preserved her from all offence. He adorns her
> with all grace. He makes her worthy of carrying him and
> receiving him into the world. He comes into her as into
> his tabernacle. He rests for nine months in her as on his
> throne. He comes to us through her.[43]

The Graces of Mary's Womb-Burden

Bérulle follows St Thomas in teaching that Christ's individual grace is really identical with his grace as Head.[44]
All that he has and does as man is a blessing for his mem-

---

[40] *Vie de Jésus* 28; 496.
[41] *Opuscules de piété* 64; 244.
[42] *Vie de Jésus* 4, 429.
[43] Ibid., 30, 504
[44] ST 3a 8, 5.

bers. 'Every action of the Son of God, his every mystery and state, infuses a certain special grace into the soul.'[45] Thus in the womb he merited specific graces for us.

> The deified incapacity of Jesus is a source of the grace of innocence, by which souls are in a holy way incapable of . . . the imperfect and defective affections of the children of Adam.[46]

The bodily incapacity of the embryonic Christ, accepted by him for love of us, is the meritorious cause in us of a spiritual 'incapacity', that is, the grace to resist the disorders of concupiscence.

According to Bérulle, there are two ways of sharing in the 'states' of Jesus' life, universal and particular. The Church universal draws special graces from each of the mysteries of Our Lord's life celebrated throughout the Church's year, above all, his Passion, death, and Resurrection. But then individual souls have the mission of being drawn more deeply into one or other of the mysteries (without, of course, losing contact with the life of Jesus as a whole).

> Jesus . . . in his states and mysteries is himself our portion, and, while giving us a universal share in him, he wants us also to have an individual share in his diverse states depending on the different ways in which he has elected us and we are devoted to him. Thus he shares himself with his children, making them partakers of the spirit and grace of his mysteries, appropriating to some his life and to others his death, to some his infancy, to others his power, to some his hidden life, to others his public life. . . . In all these different states and conditions

---

[45] Cited in Preckler (see above, note 15), 240.
[46] *Opuscules de piété* 70, 3; 262.

he gives himself to all. He gives us his heart, his grace, and his spirit.[47]

We can see this working out in the following centuries in the great men and women of French spirituality. St Margaret Mary and St John Eudes are drawn to the heart of Jesus. Charles de Foucauld finds him in his hidden life in Nazareth. St Louis-Marie sees Jesus in Mary and Mary in Jesus. Among many others, the Carmelites of Beaune, directly inspired by Bérulle, will have a special devotion to the childhood of Christ.[48] They will derive from it teaching and grace for living a life of spiritual infancy.

> The infancy of the Son of God is a passing state. Its circumstances have passed away. He is no longer a child. Nevertheless, there is something divine in this mystery that continues in heaven and that effects a similar kind of grace in the souls who are on earth, whom it pleases Jesus Christ to affect and to dedicate to this humble and first state of his person.[49]

In the great saints these particular devotions are not an exclusive attachment. In attending to a beloved part of Jesus' life, they do not lose their sense of the precious whole. They worship the Babe of Bethlehem but also the Carpenter in Nazareth, the Teacher of the Crowds, the Healer of the Sick, the Suffering Servant, the Risen Lord of Glory. And they never for one moment forget that the person whose human states these are is One of the Holy Trinity, the eternal Son of the Father. Thus the 'Little Flower' is both 'Thérèse of the Child Jesus' *and* 'of the

[47] Ibid., 188.
[48] See H. Bremond, *Histoire littéraire du sentiment religieux en France* 3/2, (1923), 218ff.
[49] *Opuscules de piété* 44, 2; 202.

Holy Face'. From womb to tomb she sees in Jesus' heart one great sweep of prodigally self-giving love.[50]

Bérulle's theology of the unborn infancy of Christ is wonderful and has much to teach a forgetful modern world, but it is not without its flaws. The refrain is always 'powerlessness', 'indigence', 'incapacity'. The colours are sombre. The general outlook on human nature is pessimistic. This is only one symptom of that Platonism in its Augustinian and medieval form that moulded Bérulle's mind and led him to stress so vigorously the nothingness of the creature in relation to Him Who Is.[51] The lessons learned from the French School need supplementing with the wisdom of St Thomas Aquinas. Human life is not just shadow and smoke. The Creator has given it its proper stability, truth, and excellence. We cannot appreciate the splendour given our humanity through assumption by the Word if we forget the beauty it already has through creation by the Word. It is not enough, then, to praise God the Son's taking of unborn childhood's poverty. We must also be thankful for his revealing and enhancing of its richness. The 'indigence' of the womb is a secret wealth; the 'incapacity' is a capacity to receive and be enriched.

The Good by Christ an Embryo

Bérulle's doctrine of the unborn Jesus, in its strengths and weaknesses, has its counterpart in the preaching of one of his English contemporaries, the most gifted Anglican divine of the Baroque age, Lancelot Andrewes (1555–

---

[50] See C. de Meester, *Dynamique de la confiance: Genèse et structure de la voie d'enfance spirituelle chez Ste Thérèse de Lisieux* (Paris, 1969), 159ff.

[51] Balthasar (see above, note 8), 14.

1626), Bishop of Winchester. St Robert Bellarmine, with
whom he clashed in controversy, regarded him as a worthy adversary, and in our own century T. S. Eliot ranked
his sermons 'with the finest English prose of their time,
of any time'.[52]

According to Nicolas Lossky, the Incarnation is 'om-
nipresent' in Andrewes' preaching. Not just the idea of
the Incarnation, but the living person of the Word incarnate is 'the centre of the message that the preacher
wants to communicate to his contemporaries'.[53] In one
of his sermons on the Nativity, he makes a magnificent
statement about the saving work of the unborn Christ.
In his astounding love for us, the Son of God becomes
an embryo in order to renew our nature at its deepest
root.

> From which His conceiving we may conceive His great
> love to us-ward. Love, not only condescending to take
> our nature upon Him, but to take it by the same way and
> after the same manner that we do, by being conceived.
> That, and no other better beseeming way. The womb of
> the Virgin is surely no such place, but He might well have
> abhorred it. He did not; *pudorem exordii nostri non recusavit*,
> saith Hilary; "He refused not that ourselves are ashamed
> of", *sed naturae nostrae contumelias transcurrit*, "but the very
> contumelies of our nature (*transcurrit* is too quick a word)
> He ran through them"; nay, He stayed in them, in this
> first nine months. I say the contumelies of our nature not
> to be named, they are so mean. So mean indeed as it is
> verily thought they made those old heretics I named, and
> others more who yet yielded Him to be Man, to run into

[52] *For Lancelot Andrewes: Essays on Style and Order* (London, 1928),
14.

[53] N. Lossky, *Lancelot Andrewes the Preacher: The Origins of the Mystical
Theology of the Church of England*, Eng. trans. (Oxford, 1991), 327.

such fancies as they did; only to decline those foul indig-
nities as they took them, for the great God of Heaven to
undergo. . . . This sure is matter of love; but came there
any good to us by it? There did. For our conception being the root as it were, the very groundsill of our nature;
that He might go to the root and repair our nature from
the very foundation, thither He went; that what had been
there defiled and decayed by the first Adam, might by
the Second be cleansed and set right again. That had our
conception been stained, by Him therefore, *primum ante
omnia*, to be restored again. He was not idle all the time
He was an embryo—all the nine months He was in the
womb; but then and there He even eat out the core of
corruption that cleft to our nature and us, and made both
of us and it an unpleasing object in the sight of God. . . .
This honour is to us by the dishonour of Him; this the
good by Christ an embryo.[54]

The goal of God's deep humbling is man's high lifting:
'His participation of our human, our participation of His
divine nature'.[55] The profits of this 'wonderful exchange'
are paid out in the sacraments. Andrewes quotes Pope
St Leo the Great: 'The same original that Himself took
in the womb of the Virgin to us-ward, the same hath He
placed for us in the fountain of Baptism to God-ward'.[56]
The Eucharist is a kind of extension of the Incarnation.
The Son of God wants to be with us and in us in the same
flesh in which he was conceived and born of the Virgin
Mary. 'This then I commend to you, even the being with
Him in the Sacrament of His Body—that Body that was

[54] Sermon IX on the Nativity in *Ninety-Six Sermons by the Right Hon-
ourable and Reverend Father in God, Lancelot Andrewes*, vol. 1, Library of
Anglo-Catholic Theology I (Oxford, 1841), 140f.

[55] Ibid., 151.

[56] Ibid., 150.

conceived and born, as for other ends so for this specially, to be "with you"; and this day, as for other intents, so even for this, for the Holy Eucharist.'[57] Our eucharistic communion with Christ is in turn 'preparative' of our union with him in the happiness of heaven: 'That as He hath been our Immanuel upon earth, so He may be our Immanuel in Heaven: He with us, and we with Him, there for ever'.[58]

Jesus Living in Mary

Bérulle's successor as Superior General of the Oratory, Father de Condren (1588–1641), wrote a prayer that sums up the dogmatic and spiritual theology of this chapter. In the last century, Gerard Manley Hopkins translated it into English.

> Jesus that dost in Mary dwell,
> Be in thy servants' hearts as well,
> In the spirit of thy holiness,
> In the fulness of thy force and stress.
> In the very ways that thy life goes
> And virtues that thy pattern shows.
> In the sharing of thy mysteries;
> And every power in us that is
> Against thy power put under feet
> In the Holy Ghost the Paraclete
> To the glory of the Father. Amen.[59]

[57] Ibid., 151f.
[58] Ibid., 152.
[59] The Poetical Works of Gerard Manley Hopkins, ed. Norman H. Mackenzie (Oxford, 1990), 103.

VI

CHRIST IN THE WOMB
OF THE HEART

The childbearing of the Blessed Virgin Mary has been seen by a long row of writers, from Origen to Blessed Elizabeth of the Trinity, as a model for the Church's (and thus the individual Christian's) faith and love and prayer.[1] Christ's indwelling of our hearts by grace (cf. Jn 14:23; Eph 3:17) in a certain way resembles his nine-month stay within his Mother, in her womb and beneath her heart. Through the overshadowing of the Holy Spirit, the Son of God took flesh from Mary and made his home within her. Through the same Holy Spirit, he and his Father live in the souls of the just. 'Anyone who does not have the Spirit of Christ does not belong to him, but if Christ is in you . . . your spirits are alive because of righteousness' (Rom 8:9f.). The Mozarabic liturgy sums up this theology when it prays that 'what was once carnally but singularly granted to Mary be now granted spiritually to the Church, that untroubled faith may conceive thee, the mind made free of corruption may give birth to thee, and the soul, by the over-

---

[1] The whole of this chapter is indebted to the definitive study of the subject by Hugo Rahner, S.J., 'Die Gottesgeburt. Die Lehre der Kirchenväter von der Geburt Christi aus dem Herzen der Kirche und der Gläubigen' in *Symbole der Kirche: Die Ekklesiologie der Väter* (Salzburg, 1964), 13–87.

shadowing power of the Most High, may ever contain thee.'[2]

In the Gospels, Jesus indicates that one can be spiritually a 'mother' to him through obedience to his Father.

> While he was still speaking to the people, behold, his Mother and his brethren stood outside, asking to speak to him. But he replied to the man who told him, "Who is my mother, and who are my brethren?" And stretching out his hand towards his disciples, he said, "Here are my mother and my brethren! For whoever does the will of my Father in heaven is my brother, and sister, and mother" (Mt 12:46-50).

St Augustine carefully explains that Our Lord's reply shows no disrespect for his Blessed Mother; on the contrary, it is to her greater glory. First, it proves that Our Lady's mothering of Christ is more than just a physical process. She is the human person who more than any other does the will of the heavenly Father, hears the Word of God, and does it. She is blessed because she bore Christ in her womb, but still more blessed because she heard and then guarded God's Word in her heart (cf. Lk 11:27f.). In words that will become classical, St Augustine says that Mary, 'full of faith, conceived him first in her mind and then in her womb: "Behold the handmaid of the Lord", she says, "be it done unto me according to thy word."'[3] The Virgin Mother is blessed 'because she kept the Word of God; not because in her the Word was made flesh and dwelt among us, but because she kept God's very Word,

[2] *Le Liber mozarabicus sacramentorum et les manuscrits mozarabes*, ed. M. Férotin, O.S.B. (Paris, 1912), 54.
[3] *Sermo CCXV*; PL 38, 1074.

through whom she was made, and who was made flesh in her'.[4]

The Holy Virgin shelters the Word of God in her body for nine months, but in her soul she guards him for ever. She is, therefore, the great model for everyone who has faith in Christ.

> Mary is therefore blessed because she heard the Word of God and kept it. She kept the truth in her mind longer than the flesh in her womb. Christ-truth, Christ-flesh: Christ-truth in Mary's mind, Christ-flesh in Mary's womb.[5]

Because Mary treasures the whole mystery of Jesus in her heart (cf. Lk 2:19, 51), because she loves him and keeps his word, the Son, with the Father and the Holy Spirit, makes his permanent home within her (cf. Jn 14:23).

In his encyclical *Mulieris dignitatem*, Pope John Paul II has taken up and further developed these patristic insights. Our Lord's response to the woman who acclaims him in St Luke's Gospel—'Blessed rather are those who hear the Word of God and keep it' (Lk 11:28)—diverts attention 'from motherhood understood only as a fleshly bond, in order to direct it towards those mysterious bonds of the spirit that develop from hearing and keeping God's word.' The Pope notes a connection with the twelve-year-old Jesus' words when he is found in the Temple: he wants to centre everything on 'the Father's business' (cf. Lk 2:49). Similarly, the adult Jesus wants to place motherhood 'in the dimension of the Kingdom of God and in the radius of the fatherhood of God himself'. His Mother is his first 'disciple'. Like him and with him, she does the will of the Father.

[4] *Tractatus X in Joannis Evangelium* 3; PL 35, 1468.
[5] *Sermo de Verbis Evangelii Matt. 12. 41–50* 7; PL 46, 938.

These at first sight disconcerting texts reveal, according to Pope John Paul, that the Blessed Virgin's motherhood is spiritual as well as fleshly, something utterly unique to her and yet in another way to be shared in and imitated by the whole Church.

> And so, in the redemptive economy of grace, brought about through the action of the Holy Spirit, there is a unique correspondence between the moment of the Incarnation of the Word and the moment of the birth of the Church. The person who links these two moments is Mary: Mary at Nazareth and Mary in the Upper Room at Jerusalem. In both cases her discreet yet essential presence indicates the path of "birth from the Holy Spirit". Thus she who is present in the mystery of the Christ as Mother becomes—by the will of the Son and the power of the Holy Spirit—present in the mystery of the Church.[6]

Both the Church as a whole and the individual Christian share in Mary's divine motherhood, her bearing of the divine Word. This idea lies behind the mysterious twelfth chapter of the Apocalypse of St John. The majority of the Fathers saw the childbearing Woman as a figure of the Church, while monastic authors in the Middle Ages (accompanied by a long liturgical and iconographical tradition) brought out more the Marian meaning. The truth is that the symbol applies to both Mary and the Church. The Woman is the Church, typified and personified in Mary, giving birth to Christ in his members in the world.[7] In St John's thinking, the Mother of Jesus

---

[6] *Redemptoris Mater*, n. 20. See Cardinal Ratzinger's commentary on Pope John Paul II's interpretation of these 'apparently anti-Marian texts' in the Gospels in *Johannes Paul II: Enzyklika 'Mutter des Erlösers'* (Freiburg, 1987), 123f.

[7] See I. de la Potterie, S.J., *Marie dans le mystère de l'alliance* (Paris,

is *the* Woman, a peerless individual with a representative, all-embracing mission.

St Irenaeus, the disciple of the disciple of the Beloved Disciple of the Lord, continues, like John, to link Mary and the Church. The eternal Son was conceived by the Holy Spirit in the Virgin Mary's womb, so that we might be re-born by water and the Holy Spirit in the womb of the Virgin Church.

> How were men to escape the birth of death except by being re-born through faith, in that new birth from the Virgin, the sign of salvation that is God's marvellous and unexpected gift?[8]

St Hippolytus of Rome (c. 170–c. 236), who according to tradition was a disciple of St Irenaeus (and thus an heir of the strongly John-inspired theology of Asia Minor), keeps the theme alive. In his treatise on Christ and Antichrist, he suggests that the pregnant woman of the Apocalypse is the Church, faithfully bearing and preaching the Word of God in a hostile world.

> "She was with child, and she cried out in her pangs of birth, in anguish for delivery" (Rev 12:2). These words mean that the Church will not cease to bear from her heart the Word that is persecuted by unbelievers in the world. "She brought forth a man-child, one who is to rule all the nations" (v. 5). In other words, the Church, always bringing forth Christ, the perfect man-child of God, both God and man, becomes the teacher of all the nations.

Earlier in the same work, Our Lady of the Visitation is seen as a type of the Church.

1988), 264; and H. Rahner, *Our Lady and the Church*, Eng. trans. (London, 1961), 107f.

[8] *Adversus Haereses* 4, 33, 4; SC 100, 810–12.

The first forerunner was John, son of Zechariah. He was
in all things our Saviour's forerunner and herald, proclaiming the heavenly light that had appeared in the world. He
first fulfilled the role of forerunner in his mother's womb,
after his conception by Elizabeth, in order to show, to
those who are infants in their mother's womb, the new
birth that was to take place for their sakes by the Holy
Spirit and the Virgin. When he heard the greeting given
to Elizabeth, he leapt with joy in his mother's womb in
recognition of God the Word conceived in the womb of
the Virgin.[9]

The reference to a 'new birth' is clearly to the sacrament of baptism. The argument seems to be that the Word
is conceived by the Holy Spirit and born of the Virgin
Mary in order to give men the grace of re-birth by water
and the Holy Spirit.

Origen, who as a young man went to Rome to hear the
preaching of Hippolytus, continues and extends the thinking of the Roman theologian; indeed, he gives this motif
its classical formulation. In and through the Church, the
believer is a 'mother' to Christ. The individual Christian is called to become what the Church as a whole is,
Christ's Bride and Mother, a truly 'ecclesiastical soul'.

What good is it to you if Christ came once in the flesh if
he does not also come to your soul? Let us pray that his
advent may daily take place in us, so that we can say, "It
is no longer I who live, but Christ who lives in me."[10]

The Logos is conceived in the soul in baptism and then
grows and is carried and brought to birth in a holy life.
Hugo Rahner, S.J., who in a classic study documented

[9] *Demonstratio de Christo et Antichristo* 61, 44; ed. G. N. Bonwetsch
and H. Achelis, GCS 1, 2d ed. (Berlin, 1897), 41, 28f.
[10] *Homiliae in Lucam* 22, 1; ed. M. Rauer, GCS 9 (Berlin, 1959), 144.

the development of the 'divine birth' theology, sets out
the Hippolytus-Origen version of it as follows:

> In Origen, as in Hippolytus, the birth of the Logos in
> the heart represents the grace received in baptism, which
> results in the vision of God. As once Mary conceived the
> Logos through her "word of faith", so now the Church,
> and with her the individual soul, becomes, like Mary, a
> "bearer of the Logos", gives birth to the Logos in her
> heart: what once was effected by the overshadowing of
> the Holy Spirit in Mary is now repeated in the Mystical
> Body of Christ. So the Church and the individual soul, in
> this spiritual birth, become Mother of Christ; God "opens
> the maternal womb" of the Church and the soul to a mys-
> terious new birth.[11]

St Ambrose introduces Origen's insights into the Latin
tradition: Christ himself, he says, is 'the Child to whom
the person who has received the Spirit of salvation in the
womb of his heart gives birth'.[12] The practical Ambrose
gives the theme an ethical turn: the Child once conceived
by the Spirit must grow and be carried by a life of virtue.
The loss of grace is like a miscarriage.

> There are those who conceive by the fear of God and
> say: "By thy fear we have conceived and are in labour"
> (Is 26:18). But not all give birth. Not all are perfect. Not
> all can say: "We have brought forth the spirit of salva-
> tion on the earth." Not everyone is a Mary, conceiving
> Christ by the Holy Spirit, giving birth to the Word. For
> some people abort the Word before they give birth. Some
> have Christ in the womb, but they have not yet formed
> him. . . . Do the will of the Father if you want to be a
> mother of Christ. Many have conceived Christ and not

[11] Hugo Rahner, *Symbole der Kirche*, 32.
[12] *Enarrationes in XII Psalmos Davidicos* 47, 10; PL 14, 1150B.

given him birth. She therefore who gives birth to justice gives birth to Christ. She who gives birth to wisdom gives birth to Christ. She who gives birth to the
Word gives birth to Christ.[13]

Through instructing and baptizing him, St Ambrose
was a spiritual father to St Augustine. Without doubt,
part of his patrimony was the notion of 'Christ in the
womb of the heart'. For Augustine, Mary is the purest
pattern of the Christian believer. What took place his-
torically in her body is to be repeated unceasingly in the
believer's soul. More precisely, her faith, which was the
core of her virginal motherhood, is to be reproduced in
the believer: 'faith in the mind, Christ in the womb'.[14]
She first conceived the Word in her heart by faith before
conceiving him in her womb according to the flesh.

> The Mother carried him in her womb; let us carry him
> in our hearts. The Virgin was pregnant by Incarnation;
> let our breasts be pregnant with faith in Christ. The Vir-
> gin gave birth to the Saviour; let our souls give birth to
> salvation, let us give birth to praise. Let us not be barren.
> Let our souls be fruitful for God.[15]

This symbolism will become classical in the Latin tradition. Hugo Rahner's judgement is correct: 'For the divine birth, too, Augustine is master.'[16] St Bede transmits
the doctrine to the Middle Ages. The Holy Virgin, carrying the Word incarnate beneath her heart across the
mountains of Judaea, is the prototype of the soul bearing
Christ through the ups and downs of human life.

[13] *Expositio Evangelii secundum Lucam* 10, 24–25; CCSL 14, 352f.
[14] *Sermo CXCVI (In Natali Domini XIII)* 1; PL 38, 1019; *Enarrationes in Psalmos* 67, 21; CCSL 39, 884.
[15] *Sermo CLXXX (In Natali Domini VI)* 3; PL 38, 1006.
[16] H. Rahner, *Symbole der Kirche*, 63.

This furnishes a type and an example: every soul which
conceives the Word of God in the mind immediately scales
lofty peaks by the path of love.[17]

St Bernard of Clairvaux develops the idea of a spiritual advent of Christ in the soul. There are, he says,
three comings of Christ—to men (in the Incarnation),
into men (by grace), against men (on the Last Day).[18] In
the first he came in flesh and weakness, in the second
in spirit and virtue, in the third in glory and majesty.[19]
The second advent takes place, according to the Lord's
promise, when a man loves him and 'keeps his words'
(cf. Jn 14:23). When there is this inner hospitality, 'the
Son will come to you with the Father, the great Prophet
will come to you to rebuild the Jerusalem of your souls
and make all things new.'[20] (There is an echo of this in
one of Balthasar's aphorisms: 'A God who for thirty years
was a carpenter and builder will also make good the ruins
of my soul.')[21]
The Schoolmen receive the theology of the spiritual
womb from their patristic and monastic predecessors. In
the treatise 'On the Five Festivals of the Child Jesus' of
St Bonaventure, the soul shares spiritually in all the mysteries of Christ's childhood, including his nine months

[17] *In Lucam* I; CCSL 120, 35.
[18] *In Adventu Domini Sermo III* 4; *Sancti Bernardi Opera*, vol. 4, ed.
J. Leclercq, O.S.B. and H. Rochais (Rome, 1966), 177.
[19] *In Adventu Domini Sermo V* I; 188.
[20] Ibid., 3; 189. Cf. Guerric of Igny: 'If your whole being abides in
the midst of silence, the almighty Word will secretly come down upon
you from the Father's throne' (*De Adventu Domini Sermo IV* 2; SC 166,
138).
[21] *Das Weizenkorn: Aphorismen* (Einsiedeln, 1953), 51.

in Mary.[22] St Thomas Aquinas, in his little work 'On the Humanity of Jesus Christ', reproduces Bede's idea: Mary is the model of all the souls which form and give birth to the eternal Word in their hearts.[23] This is the tradition that Eckhart and the German mystics take up. The Dominican Johann Tauler (c. 1300–1361) speaks of a threefold birth of Christ: eternal in God the Father, temporal in the Holy Virgin, spiritual in the Christian.[24]

Five hundred years later, in Victorian England, the tradition of Christ's birth in the soul is alive and well. In his poem on 'The Blessed Virgin Compared to the Air We Breathe', Gerard Manley Hopkins reminds us that if the believing and loving soul is a mother to Christ, she is a mother-in-the-Mother. Our Lady helps us to conceive and carry her Son in our souls. Mary is more than an external model to us. By her motherly love and intercession, she mediates the grace of Christ, who thereby makes 'new Nazareths' and 'new Bethlehems' in us. In faith, with Mary's help, I draw her Son 'like breath' into my heart as 'new self and nobler me'.[25]

In a Latin Hymn 'To the Virgin Mother', Hopkins retrieves another theme from the tradition: Our Lady of the Annunciation, accepting the Son of God into her womb, is the model for the Christian receiving his Body and Blood in Holy Communion. He asks the Mother of God to help him welcome his divine Guest with a love like

[22] *De Quinque Festivitatibus Pueri Jesu; Opera Omnia Sancti Bonaventurae* 8 (Quaracchi, 1898), 88–98.

[23] *Opusculum LIII: De Humanitate Jesu Christi* 3.

[24] J. Tauler, *Predigten*, ed. G. Hofmann (Einsiedeln, 1979), 13f.

[25] *The Poetical Works of Gerard Manley Hopkins*, ed. Norman H. Mackenzie (Oxford, 1990), 173–76.

hers.[26] In an earlier chapter, we heard a similar prayer on the lips of John Gerson.

Not long after the death of Hopkins, St Thérèse of Lisieux (1873–1897) wrote a poem that includes a stanza on how Our Lady co-operates in Christ's eucharistic residence within us.

> O Mother dearly loved, despite my littleness,
> Like you I possess within me the Lord Almighty,
> But I do not tremble when I see my weakness.
> The treasure of the mother belongs to the child,
> And I am your child, O Mother dear,
> Your virtues, your love, are they not mine?
> So when into my heart the white Host descends
> Jesus your sweet Lamb thinks he's resting in you![27]

Everything in Mary is for sharing. She even lends the communicant the welcoming womb of her heart.

Communion and Christ-Bearing

After Holy Communion, we carry Christ within us in the sacramental species just as Mary carried him in his own species for nine months. In his 'mystagogical lectures', St Cyril of Jerusalem (c. 315–386) tells the neophytes that by receiving the Body and Blood they become 'Christ-bearers' (*christophoroi*).[28] Forty years or so later his namesake of Alexandria teaches that the Word incarnate wants to dwell within us corporeally, in the flesh, and not simply spiritually, in the Holy Spirit. He does this through the Blessed Sacrament, the 'Mystical Blessing'.

[26] Ibid.
[27] 'Pourquoi je t'aime, O Marie', *Poésies* (Paris, 1979), 243.
[28] *Catecheses Mystagogicae* 4, 3; SC 126B, 136.

It is very true that we are united to Christ spiritually by perfect charity, by simple upright faith and by a pure and virtuous conscience. That is a conviction we cannot disavow. . . . But to dare to say that we do not have union with him of a fleshly kind flagrantly contradicts the inspired Scriptures. For it is precisely through the fact of this union according to the flesh . . . that Christ is the vine and we the branches, receiving life into us from him and through him. . . . Why does the Mystical Blessing penetrate us? Is it not to make Christ dwell there corporeally through communion and participation in his sacred flesh?[29]

According to the Schoolmen, Christ's sojourn in grace and charity in what we have called the 'womb of the heart' is the chief fruit of his sacramental presence in our bodies. In the words of the Council of Florence, 'the effect that this sacrament produces in the soul of the person who receives it worthily is to unite him with Christ.'[30]

Understanding the Tradition

To understand this delicate theology correctly, we must remember that it presupposes (and makes no sense without) the Christian doctrine of man. Human nature is a rich composite of spirit and matter, a wonderful unity of soul and body, 'a soul which expresses itself in a body, and a body informed by an immortal spirit'.[31] Thus in the Scriptures, physical organs—the reins, the bowels, the heart—become symbols of spiritual faculties. In the tradition we are considering, following the same principles, the womb is the symbol of the soul.

[29] *In Joannis Evangelium* 10, 2 (cf. Jn 15:1); PG 74, 341A–341C.
[30] *The Decree for the Armenians* (1439); DS 1322.
[31] Pope John Paul II, *Familiaris Consortio* 11.

CHRIST IN THE WOMB OF THE HEART 115

The second point is a warning against a possible misunderstanding. Properly understood, our theme, with
its bodily imagery of the spiritual life, protects Christian mysticism from dualistic distortion. However, it has
sometimes been spoiled by a subtle spiritualism, according to which the fleshly conception and birth of Jesus
Christ are a mere 'parable' of an eternal and universal
birth of God in the soul.[32] We must therefore state un-
ambiguously that what makes possible the soul's carrying
of Christ by grace is the historical, physical childbearing
of the Blessed Virgin Mary. This, of course, as we have
seen, is in turn accompanied and preceded by her spiritual
conceiving and carrying of Christ.

The matchless grandeur of the Mother of God must not
be dissolved into symbolism. In this matter of the 'divine
birth', she is truly Mother to us, not just model. By her
faith on earth and her intercession in heaven, she opens
up for the Church a spiritual share in her motherhood.
When Jesus says in his Mother's hearing, 'Whoever does
the will of my Father in heaven is my mother' (cf. Mt
12:50), he is asking her, according to Adrienne von Speyr,
'to give up her motherly prerogative for the sake of a certain universality'.[33] He is asking her to be a mother to the
Church by allowing the Church to be a mother with and
in her. She shows herself to be our Mother by drawing us,
through her intercession, into her motherhood of faith
and obedience. Mary mothers us into mothering Christ.

Like everything else in the religion of the Incarnation,
Christ's indwelling of the soul is both fleshly and spiritual, that is to say, sacramental. The Holy Spirit, by whom

---

[32] See H. de Lubac, *Theological Fragments*, Eng. trans. (San Francisco,
1989), 66f.

[33] *Handmaid of the Lord*, Eng. trans. (San Francisco, 1985), 111.

Christ becomes present in the 'womb of the heart', is inseparable from the water and the blood (cf. 1 Jn 5:8). He never takes us away from, but only into ever closer union with, the flesh-and-blood reality of the incarnate, crucified, and risen Lord. That is why, as the nineteenth-century theologian M. J. Scheeben suggests, transubstantiation is the supreme instance of his operation.

> Although the Holy Spirit is sent by the Son and comes to us in the Son, he is, by the strongest of appropriations, also the channel through which the Son is brought to us. As the aspiration terminating the Son's love, he urges the Son to deliver himself up to us in the Incarnation and the Eucharist. As the flame issuing from the mighty ardour of the Son in his work of sanctification and unification, in the womb of the Virgin he brings about the origin, the hypostatic union, and the resulting holiness of the Son's human nature and in the Eucharist effects the conversion of earthly substances into the Son's flesh and blood.[34]

Pope John Paul II makes a similar point in *Dominum et vivificantem* when he says that Christ's saving presence and action in us is accomplished by the Holy Spirit 'in the sacramental reality', supremely in the Eucharist—'in the Sacrifice and in Communion'.[35]

Thirdly and finally, the tradition of the mystical carrying of Christ highlights the favoured status of womanhood as an image of the creature's proper attitude towards God. The soul is always analogically feminine—bridal towards the Bridegroom, motherly towards the Child. To quote the Holy Father again, ' "being the bride", and thus the "feminine" element, becomes a symbol of all that is

[34] *The Mysteries of Christianity*, Eng. trans. (London and St Louis, 1946), 529.
[35] *Dominum et vivificantem* 61.

human.'[36] Pregnancy in particular is dense with spiritual lessons: being 'with child' is the model of being 'with Christ' in faith, hope, love, in humble service and deepest prayer. Having come, with the Father and the Holy Spirit, to make his home within me, Christ wants to remain *sub tectum meum*, 'under my roof', the king and centre of my heart. Obedience to God, formed by loving contemplation and flowering into loving action, is unending pregnancy, perpetual birth.

> The Son of God wants to take bodily form in all and from all who as his brothers and sisters are like him in spending themselves as he did in doing the Father's will.[37]

[36] *Mulieris dignitatem* 25.
[37] Hans Urs von Balthasar, *Christlich Meditieren* (Freiburg, 1984), 59.

VII

OUR LADY OF THE SIGN
THE LITURGY AND SACRED ART

In her liturgical year, the Church lives through all the mysteries of the life of Jesus, drawing from each a specific grace and lesson. As the Fathers of the Second Vatican Council declared in their Constitution on the Liturgy:

> Holy Mother Church believes that she must celebrate the saving work of her divine Bridegroom, by sacred commemoration, on certain days throughout the course of the year. Each week, on the day she has called the Lord's Day, she keeps the memory of his Resurrection. She also makes an annual commemoration of the Resurrection, together with the Lord's blessed Passion, at Easter, the greatest solemnity of all. What is more, in the course of the year, she unfolds the whole mystery of Christ from his Incarnation and Nativity to his Ascension, to the day of Pentecost and the expectation of the Lord's blessed and hoped-for return. In recalling in this way the mysteries of the redemption, she opens up to the faithful the riches of her Lord's powers and merits, so that these are in some way made present for all time, and the faithful are enabled to lay hold of them and be filled with the grace of salvation.[1]

The life of Christian monks is centred on the daily worshipping 'work of God'. It is, therefore, not sur-

---

[1] *Sacrosanctum Concilium* 102; *Decreta*, 47.

prising that they have thought longest and most deeply about the meaning of the calendar. The English Cistercian, St Aelred of Rievaulx (1109–1167), suggests that it is through the renewal and representation in the Mass of Our Lord's Sacrifice on the Cross that we become contemporary with all the mysteries of his life.

> When he handed the sacrament of his Body and Blood to his disciples, he said to them, "Do this in commemoration of me." For this reason the festivals were instituted in the Church, so that, as we represent his Nativity, Passion, Resurrection, and Ascension, all the kindness, sweetness, and charity that he shows us in all these things may always be recent in our memory.[2]

The mystery of Jesus' life in Mary's womb is always 'recent' in the Church's memory. Every evening she sings the Magnificat, the song of the Logos-carrying Virgin, in order to share more fully in her attitude of gratitude and obedience. And at the end of each year, in preparation for the Saviour's birthday, she enjoys a month's contemplation of the same mystery.

Advent

During the season of Advent, particularly its last week, the Church identifies herself with the expectant Mary, the most perfect model and embodiment of the hope of God's people: Israel's past yearning for the Messiah, the Church's present longing for the Saviour's Second Coming. In the Ambrosian liturgy, the Annunciation has always been commemorated on the Sunday before Christmas, which, together with the whole of the last week in Advent, is said to be *de exceptato* (that is to say, 'of the

[2] *Sermo VIII in Annuntiatione B. Mariae*; PL 195, 251B–251C.

[Virgin's] receiving [or conceiving]').[3] In the Tridentine Missal, a Mass of 'Our Lady's Expectation' could be celebrated on December 18, and now in the revised Roman liturgy, the mysteries spread out through the year—the Annunciation and Visitation—are celebrated during the last week before the Nativity.

All the imagery of the Fathers enters into the Advent prayers and hymns of the Breviary and Missal of Pope Paul VI. Take, for example, the collect for December 20.

> O God, at the message of an angel, the immaculate Virgin received thine ineffable Word and became the house of the Godhead, filled with the light of the Holy Spirit. Grant, we beseech thee, that, after her example, we may humbly cleave to thy will.

In St Ambrose's hymn, sung at the Office of Readings during the second part of Advent, Mary's womb is both temple and nuptial chamber.

> The Virgin womb that burden gained
> With virgin honour all unstained.
> The banners there of virtue glow;
> God in his Temple dwells below.
>
> Forth from his chamber goeth he,
> That royal home of purity,
> A giant in twofold substance one,
> Rejoicing now his course to run.[4]

The Feast of the Visitation

The Visitation is one of the few feasts of Our Lady to have its origins in the Latin Church. It was first cele-

---

[3] Cf. F. Cabrol 'Annonciation', *Dictionnaire d'archéologie chrétienne et de liturgie* 1/2, 2249.

[4] *The English Hymnal* (London, 1933), no. 14, 23.

brated in the thirteenth century, when it was introduced
into the calendar of the Franciscan Order at the instiga-
tion of St Bonaventure. The decision to extend it to the
universal Church was made by Pope Urban VI in 1389.
His hope was that the Christ-bearing Holy Virgin might
'visit' the Church anew to put an end to the Great Schism
and preserve Christ's Mystical Body in peace. Urban's
successor, Boniface IX, confirmed the decision, though
it was only accepted by that part of the Church that was
under his obedience.

> The human tongue suffices not to express the praises of so
> great a Virgin, nor can the saints fully extol with worthy
> proclamations of praise her in whose virginal palace he
> whom the heavens could not contain found shelter.[5]

The office hymn for Lauds of the Visitation (in the revised Roman Breviary) dates from the sixteenth century.
The people of God speak in the person of St Elizabeth
and ask the Mother of God to visit the Church with her
love and intercession.

> Salute the Church upon the earth
> That hearing now thy voice so dear
> Her heart may rise in joyfulness
> At knowing Jesus Christ is here.[6]

The Post-Communion of the Mass of the day takes up
the Eucharistic analogy that we have several times noted
in the tradition.

> Grant that as the Baptist joyfully leapt to greet thy Son
> hidden in his Blessed Mother's womb, we may rejoice to
> know his presence in this sacrament.

[5] O. Rinaldi, *Annales Ecclesiastici* 7 (Lucca, 1752), 512.
[6] *Te Decet Hymnus: L'innario della 'Liturgia Horarum'* (Vatican City,
1984), 171.

Masses of Our Lady

In 1987 the Congregation for Divine Worship published
a *Collection of Masses of the Blessed Virgin Mary*, in which
Our Lady's place in the mystery of Christ and his Church
is celebrated under many names and titles. With regard
to the subject of this book, there is a Mass of the 'Blessed
Virgin Mary, Temple of the Lord', in which her enshrin-
ing of the God-Man is seen in both its bodily and spiritual aspects. The prefatory note for this Mass explains
the significance of its title:

> The Blessed Virgin . . . is called a "holy temple" for a
> special reason: she carried the Son of God himself in her
> immaculate womb and became true temple of true God,
> [and] because she guarded the Word of God in her heart
> (cf. Lk 2:19, 51), loved Christ ardently and faithfully kept
> his words, the Father and the Son, as the Lord himself had
> promised, came to her and made their home with her (cf.
> Jn 14:23).[7]

The collect prays that we, too, may be temples of God.

> O God, who, in the virginal womb of Blessed Mary,
> didst ineffably fashion a holy temple for thy Son, grant
> that, faithfully guarding the grace of our baptism, we may
> worship thee in spirit and truth, and be worthy to be made
> a temple of thy glory.[8]

Elsewhere in the collection, the womb of Mary is described in a traditional way as a bridal chamber.[9]

---

[7] *Collectio Missarum de Beata Maria Virgine* I (Vatican City, 1987), 92.
[8] Ibid., 93.
[9] Ibid., Preface of the Christmastide Mass of Mary, Mother of the
Saviour, 240.

Jesus in Mary: Byzantine Praise

The name of the Mother of God is found on almost every page of the Byzantine liturgical books.[10] In every sacrament and office, in the celebration of each mystery of Christ's life, the Panagia is present in and with the Church to intercede, to contemplate and worship. Her bearing of the Father's consubstantial Son for nine months in her womb is indelibly imprinted on the liturgical consciousness of the East.

> When [the Byzantine hymnographers] sing that the immense God has been received into the Virgin's womb, that the Indescribable has taken the form of a slave, they are contemplating the Word incarnate in his Mother's womb. It is as if their meditation on the Incarnation was stopped in its tracks by this ineffable reality. The immensity of the mystery—God made man from the Virgin's most pure blood—overwhelms them and enraptures all creation: "Without leaving the womb of the everlasting Father, he dwells in the womb of the pure Virgin, and he who was without mother comes to be incarnate without father, God who reigns in righteousness. Strange and ineffable is the generation of him who is without genealogy!"[11]

It is especially in the celebration of the eucharistic sacrifice that the Greek Church pours out its praise of the womb of the Virgin. During the anaphora of St Basil, as the priest prays silently, the choir sings this loveliest of hymns:

> In thee rejoiceth, O thou who art full of grace, every created being, the hierarchy of the angels and all mankind.

[10] J. Ledit, *Marie dans la liturgie de Byzance* (Paris, 1976), 11ff. and passim.
[11] Ibid., 161.

O consecrated temple and paradise beyond all sensing, glory of virgins, of whom God, who is our God before all the ages, was incarnate and became a little child. For he made of thy womb a throne, and thy belly did he make more spacious than the heavens. In thee doth all creation rejoice, O thou who art full of glory, glory to thee![12]

This linking of the Christ-bearing Mary with the Eucharist is characteristic of all the Eastern rites. In 1987, during the Marian Year, in a homily at a celebration of the restored Armenian liturgy, Pope John Paul II quoted this acclamation: 'Incorruptible Virgin Mary, Holy Church proclaims you Mother of God: from you we have been given the immortal Bread and the Chalice of joy.'[13] The Syro-Maronite rite speaks in the person of Jesus:

The Father sent me, the incorporeal Word, and the womb of Mary, like fruitful earth, has received me like a delightful grain of wheat. And now the priests bear me in their hands above the altars. Alleluia.[14]

In the Akathist hymn of the Byzantine rite, now an indulgenced prayer for all Catholics, the Theotokos is praised as the fulfilment of all the holy places of the Old Testament.

All who hymn thy childbearing praise thee, Mother of God, as an animate temple, for in thy womb dwelt the Lord who holds all things in his hand. He it was who sanctified thee, glorified thee, and taught all to cry out to thee:

[12] *Service Book of the Holy Orthodox-Catholic Apostolic Church*, 3d ed. (New York, 1956), 108.
[13] *Liturgie dell' oriente cristiano a Roma nell'Anno Mariano 1987–88: Testi e studi* (Vatican City, 1990), 143.
[14] Ibid., 276.

Hail, tabernacle of God and the Word!
Hail, greater holy of holies!
Hail, Spirit-gilded ark!
Hail, treasury of unexhausted life![15]

Similar imagery is found in all the Marian feasts of the East. For example, on her Nativity (September 8) she is called 'the Bridal Chamber of the Light', 'the habitation of the King and Maker of all', 'the holy Temple, the Receiver of the Godhead'.[16] The 'Entry of the Most Holy Theotokos into the Temple' (November 21), which commemorates the child Mary's presentation by her parents in the sanctuary, abounds in ecstatic paradoxes and delighted ironies.

Into the holy places the holy of holies is fittingly brought to dwell, as a sacrifice acceptable to God. . . . O ye gates of the sanctuary, into the holy of holies receive ye a Virgin, the spotless Tabernacle of God the Almighty. . . . Anne, truly blessed by God's grace, led with gladness into the Temple of the Lord the pure and ever-Virgin, who is full of grace, and she called the young girls to go before her, lamps in hand. "Go, Child", she said, "to him who gave thee unto me. . . . Go into the place which none may enter: learn its mysteries and prepare thyself to become the pleasing and beautiful dwelling-place of Jesus, who grants the world great mercy." The most holy Virgin, Temple that is to hold God, is dedicated within the Temple of the Lord. . . . Dwelling-place of God, the Theotokos Mary, three years old after the flesh, is offered in the holy Tem-

[15] *Hymnus Acathistus*; PG 92, 1345D. Migne lists the hymn among the works of George Pisides, but it is also attributed to Sergius, seventh-century Monothelite Patriarch of Constantinople, and to St Germanus, eighth-century Catholic Patriarch of Constantinople. A reasonable case can also be made for the authorship of St Romanos (sixth century).
[16] *The Festal Menaion*, Eng. trans. (London, 1969), 166ff.

ple, and the virgins her companions, carrying lamps, go
before her. The ewe-lamb of God without spot, the dove
without blemish, the tabernacle that is to hold God, the
sanctuary of the glory, has chosen to dwell in the holy
Temple.[17]

The Ark Goes to Her Rest

The feast of 'The Dormition of Our Most Holy Lady
the Theotokos and Ever-Virgin Mary' takes up again all
the Old Testament images of divine presence. The falling
asleep and bodily Assumption are the final translation of
God's supreme Ark.

> Come, let us crown the Church with songs, as the Ark of
> God goes to her rest. For today is heaven opened wide as it
> receives the Mother of him who cannot be contained. . . .
> [The angels sing:] "Open wide your gates and receive her
> who bore the Creator of heaven and earth. With songs
> let us glorify her precious and holy body, dwelling-place
> of the Lord on whom we may not gaze". . . . For as the
> Mother of Life she has been transported into life by him
> who dwelt within her ever-virgin womb.[18]

Our Lady 'passes over to life', but she does not leave
us. Through the glorification of her body and soul, she
enjoys a unique intimacy with her brethren, her children,
in the flesh. At the Mother's end, as at the Son's beginning, there is no loss: virginity preserved in birth, soli-
darity maintained after death.

> In giving birth, O Theotokos, thou hast retained thy vir-
> ginity, and in falling asleep thou hast not forsaken the
> world. Thou who art the Mother of Life hast passed over

[17] Ibid., 164–98.
[18] Ibid., 509 and 511.

into life, and by thy prayers thou dost deliver our souls from death.[19]

The Image of Divine Beauty

In his encyclical *Redemptoris Mater*, Pope John Paul II emphasizes 'how profoundly the Catholic Church, the Orthodox Church, and the ancient Churches of the East feel united by love and praise of the Theotokos', and he speaks of her glorious icons venerated throughout the Christian East.

> They are images that witness to the faith and spirit of prayer of that people, who sense the presence and protection of the Mother of God. In these icons, the Virgin shines as the image of divine beauty, the abode of Eternal Wisdom, the figure of the one who prays, the prototype of contemplation, the image of glory: she who even in her earthly life possessed the spiritual knowledge inaccessible to human reasoning and who attained through faith the most sublime knowledge.[20]

One of the most ancient and best-loved icons of the Byzantine tradition, 'Our Lady of the Sign', shows the Theotokos with her hands extended in prayer and with the Holy Child in her womb. The 'sign' is the virginal conception and birth prophesied by Isaiah, 'the fifth evangelist':

> Therefore the Lord himself shall give you a sign. Behold a virgin shall conceive and bear a son: and his name shall be called Emmanuel (Is 7:14).

The child in the womb is the pre-eternal God. In his halo, his name can be seen: 'He Who Is', *ho ôn*. He who

[19] Ibid., 511.
[20] *Redemptoris Mater* 31 and 33.

once revealed himself to Moses in the burning bush
here shows himself from the incandescent purity of his
Mother. The Child-God's hand is raised in benediction.
'In my divine hypostasis,' he seems to be saying, 'your humanity, even in this its tiniest form, is blessed, hallowed,
given divine and everlasting worth.' The perpetual virginity of God's Mother is marked by the three stars on
her veil, two on her shoulders and one above her brow.
Before and in Jesus' birth, and for ever after, Mary is
Virgin.

> Gabriel was sent to the pure Virgin and disclosed to her
> joy past telling: "Thou shalt conceive without seed and
> shalt remain inviolate. For thou shalt bear a Son who is
> the pre-eternal God, and he will save his people from their
> sins. Such is the testimony of him who sent me to cry
> aloud to thee, O blessed Lady, 'Hail!' As a Virgin shalt
> thou bear child, and after childbirth thou shalt remain
> Virgin."[21]

The Ever-Virgin Mother of God is at prayer. She inter-
cedes for the Church. None can pray with more power
or compassion. God-with-us, our liberator from death,
is her living centre, the object of her every thought and
word and deed.

> Therefore, O most pure Theotokos, who livest for ever
> with thy Son, the King who brings life, pray without ceas-
> ing that thy newborn people be guarded on every side and
> saved from all adverse assault: for we are under thy pro-
> tection. And we bless thee in beauty and light unto all
> ages.[22]

In his commentary on a late sixteenth-century Russian
version of 'Our Lady of the Sign', in which both Mother

[21] Matins of the Annunciation, *The Festal Menaion*, 447f.
[22] Great Vespers of the Dormition, *The Festal Menaion*, 507.

and Child are encircled by mandorlas, Leonid Ouspensky suggests that the icon is a visual expression of words from the Akathist hymn that describe Our Lady as 'the fiery chariot of the Word' and 'the brightest morning . . . bearing the Sun-Christ'. The icon, like the hymn, emphasizes the 'cosmic significance of the Mother of God' and her role in the world's restitution, for she has 'renewed the whole world in her womb'.[23]

In the Holy Virgin's womb, in her flesh and through her faith, God the Word penetrates to the deepest level of matter, to the embryonic 'groundsill' (as Lancelot Andrewes says) of human existence, and makes it his own, raising it up to new excellence. And as he begins, so he continues. He descends into the lowest pit of human experience, into death, into the cruelty of the grave and the crevasse of Sheol. Then, on the third day, he rises up in the glory of body and soul. The Father has not let the flesh of his Son see corruption. In the Virgin's womb, and from the empty tomb, the transfiguration of matter and biology has been set in motion. It will only be complete on the last day. Then the Virgin-born Son of Man will do for us what he has already done for his Mother: he will conform our lowly bodies to his glorious body and make a new heaven and a new earth. Such are the high dogmas preached by the icon of the Sign.

Images of Jesus in his Mother's womb are also found in the West, albeit in works touched by the East. For example, there is the relief carved by Bartolommeo Buon in the middle of the fifteenth century for the tympanum over the principal doorway of the Scuola Vecchia di Santa

[23] L. Ouspensky and V. Lossky, *The Meaning of Icons* (Crestwood, 1983), 80.

Maria della Misericordia in Venice. Our Lady covers the kneeling members of the Guild of Mercy with her cloak. The Infant Jesus, his hand raised in blessing, is enthroned within a mandorla in the centre of the Virgin's body. In the *Madonna del Parto* of Piero della Francesca, painted in about 1460, the pregnant Virgin stands motionless in regal dignity. Her left hand is on her hip. Her right points to her womb. On either side, angels hold back heavy velvet drapes. They are unveiling and guarding an awful mystery.

Some artists have tried to depict the embryonic Christ at the moment of his conception by the Holy Spirit. In Russia, for example, there is the Novgorod Annunciation. In fifteenth-century northern Europe, paintings of the Visitation frequently make the unborn Jesus and John visible inside their mothers' bodies. In a wing of the fifteenth-century Friedberg altar, John-in-Elizabeth kneels and worships Jesus-in-Mary, who blesses him. In a panel by a follower of Konrad Witz, the meeting of the two cousins and their babies is shown alongside the Trinity. The message is clear: even in the womb, the Son is carrying out the mission given him by the Father.[24]

I must conclude with a word of caution. Delicacy of feeling and orthodoxy of understanding are essential requirements for the Christian artist, not least the man who tries to portray 'Jesus in Mary' in paint or stone. In the fifteenth century, St Antoninus, Dominican Archbishop of Florence, condemned pictures of the Annunciation that showed the Son in infant form being carried by the Dove from the heavenly Father into the Virgin's womb.

[24] G. Schiller, *Iconography of Christian Art*, vol. 1, Eng. trans. (London, 1971), plates 16 and 133.

These images, said Antoninus, are dangerously suggestive of the heresy of Valentinus; they make it look as if
Christ's body was brought down from heaven rather than
taken from the substance of the Virgin. Far from confirm-
ing the dogma of the Incarnation, they undermine it.[25]

[25] See *De Historia Sacrarum Imaginum* 2, 13, 7, 3, 14 in *Theologiae Cursus Completus*, vol. 27, ed. J. P. Migne (Paris, 1843), 66 and 213. See also D. M. Robb, 'The Iconography of the Annunciation in the Fourteenth and Fifteenth Centuries', *Art Bulletin* 18 (December 1936), 480–526.

VIII

THE WITNESS OF THREE WOMEN

The Apostolic Letter *Mulieris dignitatem* of Pope John Paul II is an historic document. Many of his predecessors have spoken of the Christian vocation of women, but never before has a Roman Pontiff presented a systematic theology of womanhood. Throughout his life, in all his work—as poet and dramatist, as philosopher and theologian, as priest, bishop, and pope—Papa Wojtyla has tried to understand more deeply the Creator's gift of sexual differentiation and complementarity, sealed and sanctified in the sacrament of matrimony.

The Holy Father speaks of those spiritual qualities that seem to be peculiarly feminine. Woman, he says, in the unity of her body and soul, is disposed by the Creator to motherhood, to the welcoming of new life. At her body's centre is a space to be occupied by another human being, a child, fruit of married love and gift of God. This physical predisposition is the foundation of the sensitivity and spiritual receptiveness that mark out the female.

> Motherhood involves a special communion with the mystery of life, as it develops in the woman's womb. The mother is filled with wonder at this mystery of life and "understands" with unique intuition what is happening inside her. In the light of the "beginning", the mother accepts and loves as a person the child she is carrying in her womb. This unique contact with the new human being developing within her gives rise to an attitude towards

133

human beings—not only towards her own child, but every human being—which profoundly marks the woman's personality. It is commonly thought that women are more capable than men of paying attention to another person and that motherhood develops this predisposition even more.[1]

The Pope's theology of woman is Marian. He looks at womanhood in the light of *the* Woman, the New Eve. The fulness of grace bestowed on her for her mission as Theotokos 'signifies the fulness of the perfection of "what is characteristic of woman", of "what is feminine"'.[2] Now since by the wonderful dispensation of God virginity and motherhood are united in Mary, there can be and is a 'convergence between the virginity of the unmarried woman and the motherhood of the married woman'.[3] The virginal bride of Christ is given an experience of motherhood in the Spirit, and the married woman can be blessed with an interior virginity.

If all this be true, it should not surprise us that it has been Catholic women who, in the last hundred years, have seen the importance of Jesus' life in the womb. We shall consider three here—one French, one Swiss, one English; one religious, two laywomen, one married, one unmarried.

The spiritual doctrine of the Dijon Carmelite, Blessed Elizabeth of Dijon (1880–1906), is centred on the indwelling of the Trinity in the souls of the just. She came to see the Advent Mary, the expectant Virgin, as the highest model of the contemplative, within whose heart Christ lives by grace and charity and prayer.

[1] *Mulieris dignitatem* 16.
[2] Ibid., 5.
[3] Ibid., 21.

It seems to me that the attitude of the Virgin during the months between the Annunciation and the Nativity is the model for interior souls, for those whom God has chosen to live inwardly, in the depths of the unfathomable abyss.[4]

The communion of the Mother with the Child is one of silent love.

Think what must have been going on in the Virgin's soul after the Incarnation, when she possessed within her the Word incarnate, the Gift of God. . . . In what silence, what recollection, what adoration she must have buried herself in the depths of her soul in order to embrace this God whose Mother she was. My little Guite, he is in us. O let us stay close to him in this silence, with this love, of the Virgin. That is the way to spend Advent, isn't it?[5]

Elizabeth wrote these words to her sister, Guite, who was a laywoman in the world. The thesis is that the soul of every believer—religious, priest, layman or woman— must have an 'Advent attitude' towards Christ, 'mothering' him within. Elizabeth links the Advent Mary with the Advent Baptist.

I love the idea that the life of the priest (and of the Carmelite) is an Advent preparing the Incarnation in souls. In one of the Psalms David sings: "A fire shall go before the Lord" (Ps 96:3). Is this not the fire of love? And is our mission not to prepare the ways of the Lord by our union with him whom the Apostle calls a "consuming fire"? In contact with him our soul will become like a flame of love, spreading through all the members of Christ's Body, the Church.[6]

[4] "Le Ciel dans la foi"; *Oeuvres complètes* (Paris, 1991), 124.
[5] Letter 183, to her sister (November 22, 1903); *Oeuvres complètes* (Paris, 1991), 513.
[6] Letter 250 to the Abbé Chevignard (November 29, 1905); 634f.

Elizabeth in the religious state and her sister in marriage both have a vocation of Christian love. We—she writes in the plural—must 'respond to our vocation and become perfect "praises of glory" of the Most Holy Trinity'.[7]

Elizabeth is summing up the tradition that reaches back, as we have seen, to the earliest Fathers of the Church, indeed to the teaching of God-made-man himself. She proves what the saints have always known: 'The first nine months of the life of Jesus are a fundamental, un-surpassable point of reference for the contemplative who seeks to enter into deepest intimacy with Jesus. With Mary, enveloped in the mantle of her faith and her love, he shares in the most interior way in the mystery of the Incarnation.'[8]

Among spiritual writers and theologians of the twen-tieth century, no one has given Christ's unborn human life more attention than Adrienne von Speyr (1902–1967), who combined the natural knowledge of a married woman and medical doctor with the supernatural wisdom of a mystic.[9] For the Virgin Mother, she says, the nine months is a time for the 'mixed life' of prayer and active service.

> Mary's pregnancy is a period of unbroken contemplation, of continual attention to the Son. And yet it is a time of action, for she went to Elizabeth in order to bring the Son to her, the gift she had received from God to hand on to others.[10]

[7] 'Ciel dans la foi', 125.

[8] Fr.-M. Léthel, O.C.D., Introduction to Marie-Eugène, O.C.D., *La Vierge Marie, toute Mère* (Venasque, 1988), 17.

[9] See Hans Urs von Balthasar, *First Glance at Adrienne von Speyr*, Eng. trans. (San Francisco, 1981).

[10] *The Handmaid of the Lord*, Eng. trans. (San Francisco, 1985), 53.

For the Son, too, life in the womb is a time of prayer: he prays simply by being to the full and most perfectly the real human child he has become, by surrendering, with whatever level of human freedom he possesses, his newly taken humanity, his freshly conceived infancy, to his heavenly Father. This prayer in the womb, says Adrienne, is like his prayer on the Cross:

> On the Cross he surrenders his spirit to the Father, in the womb his body. This body, which he has only just assumed, which means a new experience for him, he offers to the Father together with the joy he feels in it. And, though he is God, he is now a human being and a child, with no experience as yet of the world; he stands at the very beginning of human experience. And so he brings this body to the Father like a little child showing off his new clothes. He respects this body very highly, because it will give him access to the earth. Through it he will win back men to the Father.[11]

Adrienne here breathes new life into the theology of the 'first moment of the Incarnation', which, as we have seen, was considered before her by, among others, St Thomas Aquinas and Bérulle. Adrienne's words are reminiscent of a sermon of Gerard Manley Hopkins.

> As entering church we bless ourselves, as waking in the morning we are told to lift our hearts to God, so Christ no sooner found himself in human nature than he blessed and hallowed it by saluting his heavenly Father, raising his new heart to him, and offering all his new being to his honour.[12]

[11] *Erde und Himmel. Ein Tagebuch*, 3 (Einsiedeln, 1976), 347f. (n. 2358).
[12] *The Sermons and Devotional Writings of Gerard Manley Hopkins*, ed. C. Devlin, S.J. (London, 1959), 14.

The enfolded Son prays, and so does the enfolding Mother. Together, in loving communion with each other, they pray to the Father in the Holy Spirit. Jesus prays quite literally inside her, in her womb, in the 'praying body' of this praying Mother, who 'carries him again and again to the Father'.[13] This is more than a symbol of the worshipping Church. It is the Church's beginning. Mary is 'first Church'.

There is much modern empirical evidence to confirm the intuition of common sense that the bonds established during pregnancy between mothers and their children lay the foundation—for good or ill—of the relationship that follows birth. For Jesus and Mary, too, the understanding and love of the first nine months is continued and deepened after Bethlehem. Adrienne's spiritual director, Hans Urs von Balthasar, puts it like this:

> The mysterious dialogue within the one substance during the nine months was not broken off or even just diminished. The mystery continues unchanged; the baby who leaves his Mother incomprehensibly, the man who goes off from her, remains the fruit not only of her body but also of her faith and love.[14]

Adrienne takes up one of the great themes of Catholic tradition when she says, in connection with the Visitation, that 'bearing the Lord bodily and spiritually to others, [Mary] does what the Church was to do later in distributing the Eucharist. The Lord borne by his Mother and the Lord in the Host has only one thought: to give himself without ceasing, to distribute himself among

[13] *Erde und Himmel*, 3:347f.
[14] *Christlich meditieren* (Freiburg, 1984), 61f.

men.'[15] Balthasar the theologian has made good use of the intuitions of Adrienne the mystic.

> This attitude of letting himself be borne and driven will be perfected in the Eucharist: here the Son will hand himself over to both the holy and the unholy spirit of the Church in order to stand at the disposal of men who are not ready to let themselves be determined by his grace, by his attitude of obedience. Now as a child, later on as a man, and finally as a Host, the Son will let himself be borne about as a thing that one can dispose of—and this is he who bears the sin of the world and, therefore, the world itself.[16]

The third woman witness is Caryll Houselander (d. 1954), English Catholic poet, artist, psychotherapist, spiritual theologian, mystic.[17] Her special devotion was to Christ's different modes of presence as man among men: in the Holy Virgin's womb, in the Blessed Sacrament, and in the least of his brethren. Advent has a special meaning for her, as it does for Elizabeth of the Trinity.

> Advent is the season of the secret, the secret of the growth
>   of Christ, of Divine Love growing in silence. . . .
> For nine months Christ grew in His Mother's body. By
>   His own will she formed Him from herself, from
>   the simplicity of her daily life.
> She had nothing to give Him but herself.
> He asked for nothing else.
> She gave Him herself.
> Working, eating, sleeping, she was forming His body from

[15] *Handmaid of the Lord*, 53f.
[16] *The Threefold Garland: The World's Salvation in Mary's Prayer* (San Francisco, 1982), 38.
[17] See Maisie Ward, *Caryll Houselander* (London and New York, 1962).

> hers. His flesh and blood. From her humanity she
> gave Him His humanity.
> Walking in the streets of Nazareth to do her shopping,
> to visit her friends, she set His feet on the path of
> Jerusalem. . . .
> Breaking and eating the bread, drinking the wine of
> the country, she gave Him His flesh and blood; she
> prepared the Host for the Mass.[18]

In his meditation, the Christian must give full weight to
the infancy of Christ, especially his nine months within
Mary, when she was 'the shrine of the Sacrament, the
four walls and the roof of His home'.[19] It is not a tedious
prelude to the real business of being human.

> The Infant Christ is the whole Christ. Christ was not
> more God, more Christ, more man, on the Cross than
> He was in His Mother's womb. His first tear, His first
> smile, His first breath, His first pulsation in the womb
> of His Mother, could have redeemed the world. In fact
> Christ chose the life of growth and work and suffering and
> the death on the Cross which we know, but, by His own
> choice, all this was to depend on a human being giving
> herself to Him in His infancy, giving her own humanity
> to the actual making of that infant's humanity and giving
> Him her life in which to rest.[20]

I described Caryll Houselander above as a prophet. I
stand by that definition. I believe that she received from
God a charism of insight, not only into the mysteries of
the faith but also into the present condition of mankind,
which marks her out from her contemporaries. Her conviction that theology must not neglect the mysteries of

[18] *The Reed of God* (London, 1944), 28.
[19] Ibid., 41.
[20] *The Passion of the Infant Christ* (London and New York, 1941), 21f.

Christ's infancy, not least his first nine months of human life, was part of a broader vision of the anti-child mind of the modern world. Herod is still at his bloody work.

> Herod ordered the children to be killed because he was afraid that any one of them might be Christ. Any child might be Christ! The fear of Herod is the fear of every tyrant, the hope of every Christian, and the most significant fact in the modern world. Any child might be Christ; yes, and Herod in his attempt to destroy that one Child, to eradicate the threat of the Infant from his nation, baptized a host of children in their own blood and made a legion of little "Christs", who should come unseen with heavenly weapons, flocking to the tattered and blood-soaked standard of innocence through all the ages of mankind.[21]

In the four decades since Caryll's death, Herod's fear has taken possession of whole cultures. In the 1960s and 70s a new massacre of the innocents was decreed, not this time by a Palestinian potentate, but by the parliaments of a hundred 'civilized' lands. Unborn children have been slaughtered in their millions, their torn bodies incinerated or thrown out with the garbage. Their placentas are used to make face cream for the rich.

Caryll Houselander understood well why the child is hated by Satan and his earthly hirelings. 'Any child might be Christ!' In becoming a child, God the Son united himself to every child. Every little one of the human family is a reminder of the Infant God, of the divine humility the demons so despise. Every child preaches the Gospel just by being what he is. He embodies the simplicity needed for entry to heaven (cf. Mt 18:3). He calls his parents out of self-absorption into self-giving. (That is one of the rea-

[21] Ibid., 96.

sons husband and wife cannot be fully open to each other in sexual love if they are not open to life.)

> In the service of the infant we are made whole. Every detail of our life is set by it into a single pattern and ordered by a single purpose. We are integrated by the singleness of one compelling love. It is this wholeness which alone makes possible the complete surrender to God in which is the secret of our peace. It demands of us voluntary poverty. The giving up of self, which is Holy Poverty. As long as we have something else to give, we always cling to self; but the infant lays his minute hand on that and rejects everything else. This love, austere, childlike and poor, is life-giving love.[22]

If we are truly to follow Jesus, we must be humble enough to begin our journey where he began.

> To overcome the world we must become children. To become children we must fold our consciousness upon the Divine Infant who is the centre of our being; who is our being itself; and all that we are must be absorbed in Him; whatever remains of self must be the cradle in which He lies. This is the answer to Herod in all times, the answer of St Teresa of Lisieux in our time: "the little way of Spiritual Childhood", which is the oneing of the soul with God, in the passion of the Infant Christ.[23]

Our first teacher in childlikeness is Mary, above all the expectant Mary of Advent.

> This time of Advent is absolutely essential to our contemplation too. If we have truly given our humanity to be changed into Christ, it is essential to us that we do not disturb this time of growth. It is a time of darkness, of

[22] Ibid., 48.
[23] Ibid., 93.

faith. We shall not see Christ's radiance in our lives yet; it is still hidden in our darkness; nevertheless, we must believe that He is growing in our lives; we must believe it so firmly that we cannot help relating everything, literally everything, to this almost incredible reality.[24]

Conversion is in a special sense a spiritual Advent: 'For what is conversion but the *fiat* of Our Lady echoed again and the conception of Christ in yet another heart?'.[25] St Augustine, in recounting his conversion, tells us how at first he could not humble himself to accept the humility, the littleness, of God incarnate.[26] Similarly, Caryll Houselander suggests that we must be humble enough to accept that he who for us became a child does his transfiguring work within us in a humble and hidden way.

However else Christ is manifest in our souls, His life in them must start by being simply the infant life, the small, miraculously helpless life trusted to them to foster, that it may grow.[27]

The eucharistic analogy—the link and resemblance between Christ's presence in Mary's womb and his real, true, and substantial presence under the appearance of bread in ciborium and tabernacle—runs throughout all of Caryll's writings. It is the insight we have already noted in Adrienne von Speyr and Hans Urs von Balthasar, as well as in the mystics and doctors of the Middle Ages. Just as the unborn Jesus was utterly dependent on Mary, so now the glorified Jesus, in the Eucharist, is dependent on his members on earth.

[24] *The Reed of God*, 29.
[25] Ibid., 35.
[26] See *Confessiones* 7, 18; CCSL 27, 108.
[27] *The Passion of the Infant Christ*, 20.

By His own will Christ was dependent on Mary during
Advent: He was absolutely helpless; He could go nowhere
but where she chose to take Him; He could not speak; her
breathing was His breath; His heart beat in the beating of
her heart.

Today Christ is dependent upon men. In the Host He is
literally put into a man's hands. A man must carry Him to
the dying, must take Him into the prisons, workhouses,
and hospitals, must carry Him in a tiny pyx over the heart
onto the field of battle, must give Him to little children
and "lay Him by" in His "leaflight" house of gold.[28]

The dependence of the incarnate Word—on his Mother
in her womb, on his priests in the Blessed Sacrament—
sanctifies human dependence, which the modern world
despises. Indeed, in the unborn child and the terminally
ill, it regards helpless weakness as a capital crime.

The modern world's feverish struggle for unbridled, often unlicensed, freedom is answered by the bound, enclosed helplessness and dependence of Christ—Christ in
the womb, Christ in the Host, Christ in the tomb.[29]

Far from turning us in on ourselves, the presence of
Christ in the womb of our heart is the source of our love
of neighbour. We find him in others. We bring him to
others. In her autobiography, *A Rocking-Horse Catholic*,
she describes how, in a crowded underground train, she
was given an insight into how the Son of Man waits to
be served in every suffering man.

I had long been haunted by the Russian conception of the
humiliated Christ, the lame Christ limping through Russia, begging His bread; the Christ who, all through the

[28] *The Reed of God*, 31.
[29] Ibid.

ages, might return to the earth and come even to sinners to win their compassion by His need.[30]

The man who meditates on the Child-God in the womb and worships him under the lowly accidents of bread (the supreme, the incomparable form of his presence on earth) will not be slow to find him in the smallest of his brothers.

[30] *A Rocking-Horse Catholic* (London, 1960), 138.

REVELATION IN THE WOMB

We have one final question to answer. What is revealed by Jesus in the womb? What does he disclose of God? What does he show us of man?

One of the greatest achievements of the Second Vatican Council was its demonstration that divine revelation is not a thing but a person. It is Jesus Christ himself who is 'at once the mediator and plenitude of the whole of revelation'.[1] Pope Pius XI had already said that 'in Jesus Christ, the incarnate Son of God, the fulness of divine revelation has appeared.'[2] The Council went farther and said that Christ *is* the fulness of revelation, in himself both revealer and revealed. He reveals God, and he is revealed as God. He reveals God the Father and himself as consubstantial Son in the unity of the Holy Spirit. He, the eternal and immaterial Word, has entered into time and taken flesh in order to make the Father known by human speech and deeds: 'No one has ever seen God; the only Son, who is in the bosom of the Father, he has made him known (*exêgêsato*)' (Jn 1:18). The Word incarnate is the 'exegesis' of God. The Council Fathers continue:

> Jesus Christ, the Word made flesh, sent "as man to men",
> "speaks the words of God" (Jn 3:34) and accomplishes

[1] *Dei Verbum* 2; *Decreta*, 424.
[2] *Mit brennender Sorge*; AAS 29 (1937), 150. Cf. H. de Lubac, S.J., *La Révélation divine*, 3d ed. (Paris, 1968), 44f.

the saving work that the Father gave him to do (cf. Jn 5:36; 17:4). It was therefore he himself—to see him is to see the Father (cf. Jn 14:9)—who completed and perfected revelation and confirmed it by divine testimony. He did this by his whole presence and self-manifestation: by words and deeds, by signs and wonders, but especially by his death and glorious Resurrection from the dead, and finally by sending the Spirit of Truth.[3]

Jesus is the eternal Word of the Father, and so all his human utterances and actions, silences and sufferings, are revealing, speak volumes to us of God. As Balthasar says, he uses 'the whole expressional apparatus of human existence from birth to death, including all the stages of life, all the states in life, the solitary and the social situations'.[4] His flesh, according to St Augustine, is 'like a voice' (*caro quasi vox*), eloquent of divine truth and beauty and goodness.[5] The founding Fathers of the Cistercian Order continue this line of thinking. Their ardent devotion to the sacred humanity of Christ is always trinitarian. William of St Thierry, for example, can hear the Father speaking in every human experience of the Son.

Whatever he did, whatever he said on earth, even the insults, even the spitting, the buffeting, even the Cross and the tomb, were nothing but yourself [Father] speaking in the Son, appealing to us by your love, stirring up our love for you.[6]

---

[3] *Dei Verbum* 4; *Decreta*, 425f.

[4] *The Glory of the Lord: A Theological Aesthetics*, vol. 1: *Seeing the Form*, Eng. trans. (Edinburgh, 1982), 29.

[5] Cited in Balthasar, *Theologik*, vol. 2: *Wahrheit Gottes* (Einsiedeln, 1985), 271.

[6] *De Contemplando Deo* 10: SC 61, 92f.

He who is incomprehensible and invisible, said St Bernard, wanted to be comprehended and seen. But how?

> Lying in the manger, resting on the Virgin's lap, preaching on the mountain, passing the night in prayer, hanging on the Cross, pallid in death, "free among the dead" (cf. Ps 87:6) and ruling over hell, rising on the third day, showing the Apostles the places of the nails as the signs of his victory, lastly mounting up to heaven in their presence.[7]

The same is true of the Word's first nine months as man. Even then, as truly as when he 'preached on the mountain', he was at the work of revelation; by the simplicity of his embryonic life, Christ revealed God.

The Unborn Jesus Reveals God

The revelatory work of Jesus in the womb is mysterious and silent. He reveals, first of all, simply by being who he is (the eternal Son) and what he has become (true man, a real human embryo). He reveals by the miraculous manner of his conception and birth: 'Such a birth befits a God.' The first human person privileged to receive this revelation and ponder it in prayer is the Ever-Virgin Mother. From her it is communicated to St Joseph, St John the Baptist, St Elizabeth, St Zechariah, and so, through the Apostles and evangelists, to the whole Church.

Our Lady's faith in the incarnate Word has a chronological and theological priority in the history of salvation; as Pope John Paul II says, she 'precedes' us in faith.[8] The

---

[7] *Sermo in Nativitate B. Mariae (De Aquaeductu)* 11; *Sancti Bernardi Opera*, vol. 5, ed. J. Leclercq, O.S.B. and H. Rochais (Rome, 1968), 282.

[8] *Redemptoris Mater* 6 and passim.

believing Church first exists in her. More specifically, the Church first exists in the Yes through which the Word took flesh and dwelt within her. Our Lady, 'great with child', is image and beginning of the Church that 'magnifies the Lord'.

For nine months, Mary's faith and love are incarnated in the physical and emotional experience of pregnancy. It begins, as it does for every expectant mother, with 'a blind sense of touch, with the bodily sensing of a presence'.[9] Touch, as Aristotle and St Thomas taught, is the fundamental, the unerring sense, not a deficient form of perception, but the foundation of all others. The other senses operate through a medium, but touch is, as we say, direct 'encounter'.[10] This first sensation, in which the Son of the Most High is felt deep within her body, drawing his bodily substance and sustenance from her, will not be cast aside but be incorporated into all her later seeing and hearing and holding. She knows with unique authority what it means to say that 'the Word was made flesh and dwelt among us'. And Our Lady's experience is much more than simply individual. It is utterly unique and yet absolutely Catholic: in some way, it can be shared in the communion of saints. For the sake of the whole Church, by his touch, St Thomas the Apostle, who could not at first believe, proved the bodily solidity of the risen Christ. Similarly, for us all, by her touch, Mary, who never wavered in her faith, felt within her the reality of God's taking of flesh. The mind and heart of the pregnant Holy Virgin are the beginning (and the permanent yardstick) of the Church's confession of the realism of the Incar-

[9] Balthasar, *The Glory of the Lord* I: 359.
[10] *De Anima* 3, 16; 435A–435B. Cf. St Thomas Aquinas, *Sententia super De Anima*, lectio 18.

nation. A Christology that does not share something of Mary's wonder at the *Verbum abbreviatum*, the embryonic Word within her, is destined for Docetism.

The unborn Jesus reveals (first to Mary and through her to the apostolic Church) the Trinity's 'foolish' love of mankind. God the Father so loved the world that he sent his Son in the lowliness of embryonic human flesh. Without ceasing to be omnipotent God, the Son assumes human nature in its tiniest, most powerless form. Here begins the *kenôsis*, the self-abasement of the Son of God: *non horruisti Virginis uterum*, 'Thou didst not abhor the Virgin's womb.' He humbles himself to be mothered into human life. '*O generous love*,' says Newman, 'that He who smote / In man for man the foe, / The double agony in man for man should undergo.' Yes, and that prodigally generous love first revealed itself in the Virgin's womb. Here is the centre of Mary's wondering contemplation.

The unborn Jesus reveals not only trinitarian love towards us but the love that the triune God is eternally in himself. The miraculous manner of his human conception and birth—of a Virgin Mother without a father—is a kind of mirror image of his divine and eternal generation—by the heavenly Father without a mother. The seventeenth-century Oratorian theologian Louis de Thomassin sums up patristic opinion as follows:

> Since there are two births of one and the same Word— one in divinity, the other in humanity; the former in eternity, the latter in time—this imitation, like all temporal imitations of the eternal, had to be as clear as possible. Therefore, since he was in the one case born of the Father without a mother, so in the other it was right that he should be born of a mother without a father, of a Virgin

Father and so of a Virgin Mother, in both cases virginally
and without corruption.[11]

The temporal 'imitation' of the eternal generation can
be seen with great clarity (by the eyes of faith) during
Our Lady's pregnancy. Just as the divine Father enfolds
him in his immaterial bosom (cf. Jn 1:18), so the human Mother houses him in her fleshly womb. The nine
months of 'living in Mary' constitute the human icon of
the trinitarian indwelling or 'circumincession', 'an imitation', says Balthasar, 'within the economy of salvation,
of the mystery of the Trinity'.[12] In his humanity, as in
his divinity, the Son has his 'place' in another person.
William of St Thierry describes the trinitarian 'place' as
follows:

> O Truth, reply, I beg you. Master, where are you stay-
> ing? "Come and see", he says. "Do you not believe that
> I am in the Father and that the Father is in me?" Thanks
> to you, Lord, we have found your dwelling-place. Your
> dwelling-place is your Father, and your Father's dwelling-
> place is you. Thus you are found in this place. But this
> place of yours . . . is the unity of the Father and the Son,
> the consubstantiality of the Trinity.[13]

The three divine persons are not impenetrable self-
enclosed fortresses, but fluid self-giving persons. They are

[11] L. de Thomassin, *Dogmata Theologica*, 2 (Paris, 1680), 112. St Augustine says: 'Christ has been born: as God, of the Father; as man, of
his Mother . . . of his Father without a mother, of his Mother without
a father' (*Sermon CXCIV* [*In Natali Domini XI*] 11; PL 38, 1015). St
Proclus is typical of the Greek tradition: 'An only Son cannot be born
of two fathers. He who is without mother in heaven is without father
on earth' (*Oratio IV* [*In Natalem Diem Domini*] 3; PG 61, 714B–716B).

[12] *The Glory of the Lord* 1: 339.

[13] *Oratio Domni Willelmi* 6; SC 324, 214.

'subsistent relations', three selfless selves. Each is himself in relation to the others. Each encompasses and includes the others: the Son in the Father, the Father in the Son, both in the Spirit, and the Spirit in both. They find their place in each other. Human womb-life, in which the child has his place in his mother, is beautifully adapted to the revelation of the Trinity. It is also a fitting prelude to the redemptive work of 'substitution and exchange', by which, finally, on the Cross, the Son-made-man will put himself in the place of sinful men, so that sinful men may find their place in the Father. And it looks forward to eucharistic Communion, in which, under the accidents of bread and wine, the good Jesus—Body, Blood, Soul, and Divinity—really and truly resides within us.

The Unborn Jesus Reveals Man

Jesus is the revelation of man as well as of God. Man does not fully understand his own humanity until he sees it united to the divinity in the person of the Word. This is the teaching of the Second Vatican Council:

> It is in fact only in the mystery of the incarnate Word that the mystery of man becomes truly clear. For Adam, the first man, was the type of the One who was to come, namely, Christ the Lord. Christ, the last Adam, in the very revelation of the mystery of the Father and his love, fully manifests man to himself and opens up his sublime vocation.[14]

But in what sense is man a mystery? Why does man need the light of revelation fully to understand himself? And what does the embryonic Christ reveal about man?

[14] *Gaudium et Spes* 22; *Decreta*, 709.

St Gregory of Nyssa gives us part of the answer. Man has been created in the image of God, and so in a certain way he reflects the divine incomprehensibility. ' "Who has known the mind of the Lord?" asks the Apostle (1 Cor 2:16). But I say: "Who has known his own mind?" '[15] Made in the image of God, man reproduces the unspeakable mystery of the Trinity. In one sense, says Gregory, it is easier to know the heavens than oneself.[16] In his commentary on Psalm 41, St Augustine says that man is an abyss, the deep that calls upon the divine deep 'in the roar of the waters'.[17]

The doctrine of the image of God in man is the only guarantee of an 'integral humanism'. Man is only great because God is infinitely greater. When the Creator is denied, the creature is destroyed. All the heresies of the past and the ideologies of the present claim exhaustive knowledge of man. They reduce the richness of his mysterious nature, scale him down to one or other of his parts or powers. Spiritualistic dualism (Platonic or Cartesian) makes him an imprisoned spirit, a ghost in a machine. Materialistic monism (Marxism, Darwinism, Behaviourism) sees him as an economic animal, a naked ape, a black box. Pelagianism inflates his freedom, while Calvinism and Jansenism obliterate it. Liberal Capitalism exalts the enterprising individual; Communism sacrifices the individual to the collective. Only Catholic Christian faith understands man rightly in the richness of his nature and the dignity of his person.

When the eternal Word is made flesh, the full wonder

[15] *De Hominis Opificio* 11; PG 44, 153D.

[16] *De Creatione Hominis Sermo I; Gregorii Nysseni Opera: Supplementum,* ed. H. Hörner (Leiden, 1972), 4.

[17] *Enarrationes in Psalmos* 41, 13; CCSL 38, 470.

of man's being is made plain. Man is made 'in' the image of God, but the Word *is* the Image of God, the Father's consubstantial Image. Man has therefore a special relationship with the Second Person of the Trinity: he is man's uncreated exemplar, the model from which the Father cast Adam's features. In the person of the Son, humanity becomes what the Trinity always wanted it to be. The incarnate Word 'makes clear' that man's eternal destiny, 'from before the foundation of the world' (cf. Eph 1:4), is to be conformed to him, to be a son-in-the-Son, on earth by grace, in heaven in glory, 'Those whom [the Father] foreknew he also predestined to be conformed to the image of his Son, in order that he might be the first-born of many brethren' (Rom 8:29).

It is evident that it is only through Christ, by divine revelation, that man comes to know his 'most high calling' of adoptive sonship and beatific vision. But what light does the God-Man throw on those truths about man that are known or knowable by reason?

The human intellect was not deprived of its capacity to know the truth by the sin of Adam, but it was weakened and wounded, and so it is easily lead astray by the vanities of worldly wisdom and its own concupiscent whims. Studiousness, the humble quest for knowledge, can be perverted into curiosity, the proud craving for information. Thus, by his reason's unaided light, man cannot fully grasp the 'wonder of his being' (cf. Ps 138:14). There are truths concerning his nature, in principle knowable by reason, which in his fallen condition he finds it hard to grasp. As St Thomas says, 'there is an element of falsity in most of the investigations of human reason owing to the weakness of our intellect in making judgements and to the role played by imagination. The result is that many would continue to doubt even things that have been most accurately demonstrated because they do not realize the force of the demonstration, especially when they see the people reputed to be wise teaching different things.'[18] St Thomas is speaking here about man's knowledge of God, but, with appropriate qualifications, his comments apply to man's knowledge of himself.

Because of the mysteriousness of human nature and the weakness of the fallen human intellect, there is a moral need for revelation with regard to certain naturally knowable truths about man. The most obvious example is the difference within man of matter and spirit and the intimacy of their union. Plato affirmed the spirituality and immortality of the soul but regarded the body as a prison or tomb. The soul was the essential self. Aristotle argued for the 'hylomorphic' unity of human nature but did not teach the immortality of the individual rational soul. In Greek Antiquity, there is a tantalizing perception of parts of the truth about man, but nowhere is there a balanced sense of the whole. St Augustine says that if only Plato and Porphyry had merged their doctrines of the soul, they would have both been Christians.[19] It took God in human flesh and blood to confirm the integral place of the body in our nature. As Cardinal Newman says in his *Essay on the Development of Christian Doctrine*, 'by the fact of an Incarnation we are taught that matter is an essential part of us, and, as well as mind, is capable of sanctification.'[20] Newman lists this proposition as one of the essential 'principles of Christianity' that directed doctri-

[18] *Summa Contra Gentiles* 1, 4.
[19] *De Civitate Dei* 22, 27; CCSL 48, 854.
[20] *Essay on the Development of Christian Doctrine*, new ed. (London and New York, 1960), 235.

nal development in the patristic age. For the Fathers, the hinge on which the whole faith turns is the flesh: *caro cardo salutis.*

The Greek philosophers never developed a clear understanding of human personhood. Aristotle's theory of primary and secondary substances is only the remotest preparation for the Cappadocian distinction between *hypostasis* and *ousia.* Before the trinitarian and christological controversies of the fourth and fifth centuries, *hypostasis, ousia, physis, prosôpon (persona)* had a bewildering range of everyday and philosophical meanings. 'Even linguistically, it needed a God, an incarnate God, to bring "person" (*persona*) to the fore. Until Christian times, in the language of Rome, it meant an actor's mask.'[21] It took the revelation of the three divine persons in and by the incarnate Son to open up the meaning and worth of human personhood. The concept of person is one that the mind can acquire naturally. It corresponds to a universal human experience; any man can understand the difference between asking 'Who is it?' and 'What is it?' And yet 'it could never have been fully elaborated without the decisive contribution of the Christian dogmas of the Trinity and of the Incarnation of the divine Word.'[22]

Balthasar has formulated our argument as follows:

Much of what is deepest in man, because of his estrangement from God, is submerged and forgotten. Only

---

[21] Christiane Morati cited in H. de Lubac, S.J., *Foi chrétienne,* 2d ed. (Paris, 1970), 318. Cf. the International Theological Commission on 'The Interpretation of Dogma', *Origins* (May 17, 1990), 12.

[22] Y. Floucat, *Pour une philosophie chrétienne: Éléments d'un débat fondamental* (Paris, 1981), 43.

through the Incarnation is it brought back to the light of remembrance and human self-understanding.[23]

Now, according to Balthasar, this is particularly true of childhood (at all its stages). 'Everywhere outside of Christianity the child is sacrificed automatically.'[24] Only in the light of God-made-child is childhood understood and rightly cherished. Only in the light of God-made-child at conception is life in the womb grasped in all its grandeur.

'Recapitulation' in Jesus Christ

In him [say the Fathers of the Second Vatican Council] human nature was assumed, not annihilated, and so, by that very fact, in us, too, it has been raised up to a sublime dignity. For by his Incarnation, the Son of God has in some fashion united himself with every man.[25]

It is truly our common human nature that the Son of God has made his own. He who is of one substance with the Father in divinity has become of one substance with his Mother and with us in humanity. When we say 'human nature', we mean not only our general make-up (material body and rational soul) but also our life, our earthly odyssey from conception to the last breath. Every state and stage of human existence has, therefore, been 'raised up to a sublime dignity', and every human being has been 'united' to the Son of God, made his kinsman and fellow. As St Irenaeus says, he has recapitulated us all: summed us up and given us a new beginning. 'He passed through ev-

[23] Balthasar, *Wenn Ihr nicht werdet wie dieses Kind* (Ostfildern, 1988), 21.

[24] Balthasar, *Das Ganze im Fragment: Aspekte der Geschichtstheologie*, new ed. (Einsiedeln, 1990), 282.

[25] *Gaudium et spes* 22; *Decreta*, 710.

ery age, becoming an infant for infants, thus sanctifying infants.'[26] St Leo makes the same point à propos of the Holy Innocents (sanctified by the Babe of Bethlehem):

> He crowned the infants with a new glory, and by his own early days he consecrated the beginnings of little ones, so that he might teach us that no man is incapable of the divine mystery.[27]

By becoming man at his conception, the Son of God has united every unborn child to himself and made all womb-life not simply sacred but divine, worthy of God himself. He has consecrated 'our beginnings'. Even the microscopic stage of human existence is 'capable of the divine mystery'. In the womb of Our Lady, God the Son has ennobled the very qualities that the Prometheanism of modern culture dismisses as incompatible with complete humanness—dependence, helplessness, weakness.

> The Son of God, by becoming thus son of a mother, accepts with regard to humanity the dependence that humanity had refused with regard to God. The Son of the Father, by becoming Son of Mary, accepts a humanity that is not only received but dependent, limited, determined by the existence of his Mother, a humanity that was hers before it was his, which only becomes his through her.[28]

The Spirit-filled Messiah first preached 'good news to the poor' (cf. Is 61:1; Lk 4:18–19), first embraced poverty and made the poor his special brethren, at the moment of his Incarnation.

> You do not need to be reminded how gracious our Lord Jesus Christ was; how he impoverished himself for your

---

[26] *Adversus Haereses* 2, 22, 4; SC 294, 220.
[27] *In Epiphaniae Solemnitate Sermo II* 3; SC 22B, 224.
[28] L. Bouyer, *Le Trône de la sagesse*, 221.

sakes, when he was so rich, so that you might become rich through his poverty (Knox, 2 Cor 8:9).

It would be 'impoverishment' for the Creator of the universe to assume the nature of the highest of the seraphim, but to enter human life at its beginning, when it is most vulnerable, is an act of divine mendicancy. 'Dwindled to infancy', he comes begging shelter, the warmth of his Mother's heart and body, and with immaculate generosity she gives it, as Hopkins says, unbounded 'welcome in womb and breast'.[29]

I shall try to define more exactly what I mean by God the Son's 'poverty' in the womb. The unborn child is not poor by analogy with the materially deprived; the materially deprived are poor by analogy with the unborn and the dying: 'Naked I came from my mother's womb', says Job, 'and naked shall I return' (Job 1:21). But the poverty of the unborn child is also a richness (this is what Bérulle failed to see): it is an unhindering openness to the wealth of life pouring into his veins from his mother. The embryonic Christ is poor and rich in this sense. The Son who eternally receives the divine nature from God the Father receives in time human nature from his Mother. He takes in all that she has to give, flesh from her bodily substance, love from her immaculate heart. In the light of the incarnate Word, we begin to understand the paradoxes of the Gospel: the poor in spirit possess the Kingdom (cf. Mt 5:3); they have nothing, and yet they possess everything (cf. 2 Cor 6:10).

The embryonic Christ, simply by being what he is, proclaims in advance his later teaching: 'Unless you turn and

[29] Gerard Manley Hopkins, 'The Blessed Virgin Compared to the Air We Breathe', *The Poetical Works of Gerard Manley Hopkins*, ed. Norman H. Mackenzie (Oxford, 1990), 173.

become like little children, you will never enter the kingdom of heaven' (Mt 18:3). God took the 'little way' when he became man. He came and lay 'all so still where his Mother was'. Without throwing off his divine grandeur, he took the smallest form of human life; he became a Spirit-fashioned and Spirit-filled 'zygote'. He is the first realization of his parable of the mustard seed (cf. Mt 13:31–32). The Father's Word is sown by the Holy Spirit as a tiny grain of humanity in the Virgin-field, and then, having reached the ripeness of manhood, having taught and healed, having suffered and died, he becomes in the Resurrection the mighty Tree of Life housing angels and men and all creation in his arms. ('He is that Mustard tree', says Newman, 'which was destined silently to spread and overshadow all lands.')[30]

In the manner of his Incarnation, God exposes the folly of self-aggrandizement and proves the wisdom of humility. He could have assumed human nature in adult form and proceeded swiftly to his task, but he chose not to. He took the low road, the slow route of human growth from conception, blessing every staging-post on the highway. As St Irenaeus understood so well, patience is an attribute of God before it is a virtue of man.[31]

The Holy Eucharist continues the little way of the Incarnation. The great God who became a baby in Mary's womb here gives his whole mighty self—Body, Blood, Soul, and Divinity—in the tiny form of the Host. And he invites a Mary-like response of wholehearted welcome. The Mother of God stands by every communicant at

[30] John Henry Newman, 'The Visible Temple', *Parochial and Plain Sermons*, new ed. (San Francisco, 1987), 1352.

[31] See *The Scandal of the Incarnation: Irenaeus 'Against the Heresies'*, Eng. trans. (San Francisco, 1990), 72f.

the altar. Both Christ's gift and the human response pass through her motherly love. Father Jean Galot, S.J., in one of his early books, speaks thus of the two-way flow of the Handmaid's help.

> Mary is the mediatrix of the grace of Holy Communion. She is, of course, mediatrix of all graces, but in Holy Communion this mediation assumes a special form. The Eucharist is the only sacrament in which Mary can give back her Son in person, particularly the body once formed in her womb. In the Eucharist she renews her Yes to the Incarnation and deploys all her motherly love of humanity. Her motherly affection wants to nourish her children, to give them a spiritual food enabling them to be more like her Son, to identify more completely with him. As well as collaborating in the gift of the Eucharistic Christ, Mary helps us welcome it. In the Incarnation she was the perfect model of welcoming the Word made flesh; she received Christ with all the enthusiasm of her faith and all the abandonment of her love. . . . Consequently, the Virgin is the right person to promote the dispositions of welcome in the communicant.[32]

As St Irenaeus taught in the second century, as St Cyril of Alexandria re-affirmed against Nestorianism, orthodox Christology, Mariology, and eucharistic doctrine stand and fall together.

The Revelation of Ethics

In his 'Nine Propositions on Christian Ethics', written originally for the International Theological Commission, Hans Urs von Balthasar states that Jesus himself is 'the concrete and plenary norm of all moral action'. He reveals moral truth, not just by his words, but by his whole hu-

---

[32] J. Galot, *Eucharistie vivante* (Paris, 1963), 271.

man life and activity. He reveals the Father's Law, man's path to final happiness, and lives it out by his obedience unto death.

> Christian ethics must be elaborated in such a way that its starting-point is Jesus Christ, since he, as the Son of the Father, fulfilled the complete will of the Father (= everything that must be done) in this world. He did this "for us", so that we might gain our freedom through him, the concrete and plenary norm of all moral action, to accomplish God's will and to live up to our vocation to be free children of the Father. . . . The norm of the concrete existence of Christ is both personal and universal, because in him the Father's love for the world is realized in a comprehensive and unsurpassable way. This norm, therefore, embraces all men in their different ethical situations and unites all persons (with their uniqueness and freedom) in his person. As the Holy Spirit of freedom, it also hovers over all men in order to bring them to the Kingdom of the Father.[33]

By his human words and deeds, by his acts of human obedience (from his coming into the world), the incarnate Word confirms and sheds new light on those moral

---

[33] *The International Theological Commission: Texts and Documents 1969–1985* (San Francisco, 1989), 108f. St Bonaventure presents the same idea in a striking metaphor taken from medieval diplomacy. The Word made flesh is humanity's universal (and concrete) norm. 'We cannot pretend that we do not know what God wills. For we have a legate *a latere*, who knows the monarch's will. He has become in his own person a radiant revelation and general ethics and universal training in morality. Thus our way of acting must not be different from Christ's. Our way of living must not be different from Christ's. Our way of suffering must not be different from Christ's. And our way of dying must not be different from Christ's' (*Sermo II in Nativitate Domini* 1; *Opera Omnia Sancti Bonaventurae*, 9 [Quaracchi, 1901], 107).

truths that, at least in principle, any man can apprehend by the light of reason. Anyone should be able to see that the life of the human being begins at the moment of fertilization and from that moment has the right to be protected from attack. But the Catholic believer, who confesses that the Son of God became man at the moment of his virginal conception, has the greatest of all possible grounds for reverence. Unborn life has been assumed and therefore divinized by the consubstantial Word. To attack the unborn is to declare war against God.

To hold that the absolute inviolability of human life from conception has been revealed by the Redeemer in the womb is not to neglect natural law ethics. According to the teaching of the First Vatican Council, which here follows St Thomas, the requirements of the natural law, which are in principle accessible to the human mind, in the fallen condition of man can only be known with firm certitude and without trace of error from revelation.[34] As Germain Grisez says, 'the Church's teaching, based on divine revelation, gives us a motive to accept as true those norms of Christian morality for which we may not have completely satisfying arguments.'[35] What greater motive can there be for accepting the Church's teaching concerning conception and the dignity of the unborn than God the Son's acceptance, at his virginal conception by the Holy Spirit, of the embryonic and fetal state of mankind? What greater reason can we have for respecting the human person than the assumption of human nature by the

[34] ST 1a 1, 1; 1a 2ae 98, 5; Vatican I, *Dei Filius*, cap. 2; DS 3005.
[35] *The Way of the Lord Jesus*, vol. 1: *Christian Moral Principles* (Chicago, 1983), 177.

divine person of the Son? 'Wake up, O man', say the Fathers, 'to the dignity God-made-man has given thee.'

From this I conclude that the moral norms taught by the Church concerning the beginning of human life are truths of divine revelation. By his assumption of human nature at the moment of conception and his nine months in the womb, the Word of God teaches specific ethical norms. If the Child-God has hallowed all human childhood from its first beginnings, then the contracepting person's will that a possible child should not begin to be is intrinsically unholy; that is, the contraceptive act is absolutely and in all circumstances gravely sinful. Similarly, if the womb has for nine months been found worthy of the presence of God, then the attack on the unborn is an act of sacrilege, the abomination of desolation. If Christ is truly the Head of all men, united through his Incarnation to every man conceived, then he truly suffers in every act of abortion, just as he is neglected in the unfed hungry and the naked man without clothes (cf. Mt 25:42ff.). As a German woman poet has written:

> When woman fears life,
> it becomes dark on earth.
> Dread haunts every corner.
> Females of flint line up,
> rip out the besieged fruit,
> twenty-five million
> a year, from out of the guarded cradle,
> God's Son in every child.
>
> "Pregnancy product" in the refuse,
> Last scream from the plastic bag
> through the night-blackened days.
> Empty swell in hollow body
> aborted fruit of love

from sterile den of thieves.
Motherless ship of the world
How will you find atonement?[36]

Incarnation, Ethics, and Ecumenism

Catholic doctrine—Christology, Mariology, eucharistic theology, and moral theology—is a tightly interwoven tapestry; to cut away one part is to ruin the whole. The history of Protestantism is living proof of this thesis. The Reformation's rejection of Mary and the Mass has been followed, four centuries later, by the widespread abandonment of Christian morality and faith in God incarnate. A Maryless Christology has become a Christianity without Christ. Those who once refused honour to the Mother no longer worship the Son: denial of his divinity, of his virginal conception and bodily Resurrection, is *officially* tolerated throughout the Anglican and mainstream Protestant world.[37] The denominations that once cast off consecrated virginity have now discarded the ho-

[36] Maria Eschbach, *Das weisse Kleid*. Gedichte (Einsiedeln, 1986), 59. On the will to contracept as contra life, see G. Grisez et al., ' "Every Marital Act Ought to Be Open to New Life": Towards Clearer Understanding', *The Thomist* 52 (1988), 365–426.

[37] Speaking of Our Lady as 'The Tower of David', Cardinal Newman says: 'Look at the Protestant countries which threw off all devotion to her three centuries ago, under the notion that to put her from their thoughts would be exalting the praises of her Son. Has that consequence really followed from their profane conduct towards her? Just the reverse—the countries, Germany, Switzerland, England, which so acted, have in great measure ceased to worship Him, and have given up their belief in His Divinity; while the Catholic Church, wherever she is to be found, adores Christ as true God and true man, as firmly as she ever did. . .' (*Prayers, Verses and Devotions* [San Francisco: Ignatius Press, 1989], 170–71).

liness of matrimony: the 're-marriage' of divorcees and the practice of contraception (once condemned by the Reformers) are today everywhere permitted, even promoted. Those Anglican prelates who deny the virginal conception of the God-Man do not hold dear the natural conception of any man. According to the Archbishop of York, 'moral worth' does not have to be given to the whole history of a human person; and so, he concludes, experimentation on the human embryo is permissible.[38]

The doctrinal gulf between the Catholic Church and the Protestant denominations is greater than it ever has been. The abjuring of traditional Christian ethics has been accompanied by (and may well be caused by) the loss of orthodox Christology. The dogmatic and ethical vision of a Lancelot Andrewes has passed away. In their official teaching, Anglicanism and Protestantism no longer confess 'the good by Christ an embryo'.

St Joseph: Towards a New Christian Chivalry

When the triune God calls a human being to his service, he asks for an answer like the Yes by which the Holy Virgin ushered the eternal Son into her soul and womb: generous welcome followed by faithful protection. In a sense, says Balthasar, the seed of the Word is always sown as an unborn child.

> The Word-Child in his silent powerlessness can so easily and by a thousand means be rejected and aborted, almost without religious people noticing (just as human soci-

[38] In the debates in the House of Lords on the White Paper on Human Fertilization and Embryology (January 15, 1988), and on the later Bill (December 7, 1989), Dr Habgood spoke in support of experimentation on the human embryo.

ety is built upon the tacit, thousandfold murder of the
unborn, as if it were a foundation over which no words
need be wasted). The Word-Child nestles within us and
seeks safety and protection in weak human flesh. "He did
not come as a conqueror but as one seeking shelter. He
lives as a fugitive in me, in my care, and I have to answer
for him to the Father" (Bernanos).[39]

The tremendous Lion of Judah gives himself to us as
the tiny Lamb of God. Before he comes at the end in
power and with his angels, the glorified Christ comes to
us, as he did once in the womb of Mary, in the form of
littleness and lowliness: under the accidents of bread, and
then, in a different way, in the persons of the poorest—
his unborn friends and comrades, the least, the littlest of
his brethren. He wants the shelter of charity. He craves
faithful protection. Another woman poet—Elizabeth
Jennings—has heard his call.

> How can we not feel love
>   To see such helplessness?
> Our cold hearts start to move
>   With an old gentleness,
>
> Yet it is new also
>   Since we are feeling for
> A God who is to grow
>   To manhood like the poor.
>
> Listen, let Mary sing
>   Her unborn child a cry
> Such as all mothers bring
>   To their first lullaby.[40]

[39] Balthasar, *Das Ganze im Fragment: Aspekte der Geschichtstheologie*,
new ed. (Einsiedeln, 1990), 276.
[40] Elizabeth Jennings, 'The Journey to Bethlehem' in 'A Christmas
sequence', *The Tablet* 22/229 (December 1990), 1650.

The vocation of the Christian, inscribed in his baptism, is to mother the Son by obeying the Father in the Holy Spirit. We are called to conceive and shelter Christ by a life of faith, hope, and charity. In other words, we are called to be like the Virgin Theotokos, but we can only be like her if we know and love her, if we give her the honour that is her due. Only by offering her the refuge of our hearts can we imitate her in sheltering and carry-ing Christ. St John of the Cross loved the annual Christ-mas ceremony at Granada re-enacting St Joseph's and the pregnant Mary's request for lodging.

> With the divinest Word the Virgin
> Made pregnant, down the road
> Comes walking, if you'll grant her
> A room in your abode.[41]

St Joseph was the first man to grant the pregnant Vir-gin 'a room in his abode'. Before ever he sought for her the hospitality of the inn-keepers of Bethlehem, he had not been afraid to take her into his own home and heart (cf. Mt 1:24). He is the model of the chivalry of Cath-olic faith, of every knight of the helpless Word. He of-fered a house—a roof but also a lineage—to the unborn Jesus. He gives sanctuary to God incarnate and his Tem-ple. Through the prayers of his guardian, may the world come to faith in the Redeemer in the womb.

[41] St John of the Cross, *Poems*. With a translation by Roy Campbell (Harmondsworth, 1960), 107.

ABBREVIATIONS

CC   *Corpus Christianorum* (Turnhout, 1953ff.)

CM   *Continuatio Mediaevalis* (cf. CC)

CSCO   *Corpus Scriptorum Christianorum Orientalium* (Paris, 1903ff.)

Decreta   *Sacrosanctum Oecumenicum Concilium Vaticanum II: Constitutiones, Decreta, Declarationes* (Vatican City, 1966)

DS   *Enchiridion Symbolorum, Definitionum et Declarationum de Rebus Fidei et Morum*, ed. H. Denzinger, new ed. A. Schönmetzer, S.J. (Rome, 1976)

FC   *Fontes Christiani* (Freiburg, 1990 ff.)

GCS   *Die griechischen christlichen Schriftsteller der ersten drei Jahrhunderte* (Leipzig and Berlin, 1897ff.)

PG   *Patrologia Graeca*, ed. J. P. Migne (Paris, 1857–1866)

PL   *Patrologia Latina*, ed. J. P. Migne (Paris, 1844–1864)

SC   *Sources chrétiennes* (Paris, 1940ff.)

SL   *Series Latina* (cf. CC)

ST   St Thomas Aquinas, *Summa Theologiae*

INDEX

abortion, 60, 76, 141, 165–66, 167–68

Abraham, 36

Adam, 12, 20n, 58, 66–67, 89, 153, 155

Advent, 6, 120–21, 134–36, 139–40, 142–43

Aelred of Rievaulx, St, 120

Akathist (hymn), 125, 130

Ambrose, St, 25, 48, 49, 50, 109–10, 121

Ambrosian rite, 120

Anastasius of Sinai, St, 44–45

Andrew of Crete, St, 49–50, 86

Andrewes, Lancelot, 98–101, 130, 167

Anglicanism, 166, 167

animation. *See* delayed animation; immediate animation

Anne, St, 126

Antichrist, 107

antiquity, 156, 157; and body, 13–15, 46, 59; and unborn, 46–47, 59–60; understanding of conception of, 13–15, 72; and women, 46

Antoninus, St, 131–32

Annunciation, 5–6, 28–29, 36; and Church, 7, 120–21; and Eucharist, 112–13; images/icons of, 131–32

Aquinas, St Thomas, 40, 98, 112, 137, 150, 164; on conception, 14–16, 18–21; on fetal life of Jesus, 68–73, 75–78, 86; on headship of Christ, 65, 87, 95; on Jesus, 2, 18–21, 64; on man, 19–21, 155–56; on soul, 16–18

Ark of the Covenant, 27–28, 47, 52, 58–59, 86, 127

Aristotle, 9, 13–15, 150, 156, 157

Armenian rite, 125

Assumption of Mary, 56–59, 127–28

Athanasius, St, 8, 52, 70

Augustine, St: on children, 75; on humility of God incarnate, 46, 143; on Incarnation, 49n, 51n; on Jesus, 104, 148, 152n; on John the Baptist, 25–26n; on man, 154; on Mary, 54, 104, 110; and Platonism, 98, 156; on Porphyry, 46, 156

Augustus, 91

immortality, 156
Incarnation, 5–6, 20n,
    87–88, 124, 132, 137,
    161; and bridal images,
    54–56; and Eucharist,
    80, 100–101, 116; and
    Fathers, 4n, 5, 43–60;
    and Middle Ages, 61–
    63; and nature of man,
    11, 12–13, 19–20, 157;
    and Nestorius, 50–54;
    revelation in, 148, 149–
    53, 156–62; scandal of,
    46–47; and Shekinah, 29–
    33; timing of, 3, 4–5, 10;
    and unborn, 141, 164–65;
    wonder of, 6–7, 86–87,
    150–51. *See also* Holy
    Spirit; hypostatic union;
    immediate animation; Son
individual Christians, 96–97;
    dwelling of God in, 103,
    115–16, 117, 123, 134–
    35; and Eucharist, 112–
    14, 161–62; and Mary,
    103–4, 105, 109–10,
    112–13, 123, 169; and
    spiritual motherhood, 106,
    108–13, 169
infanticide, 60
inhabitation, 50–52
International Theological
    Commission, 71, 162–63
Irenaeus, St, 37, 87, 107,
    158–59, 161, 162
Isaac, 32
Isaiah, 39, 41, 128
Israel, 31, 34–35, 120;

and Mary 36–37; and
Shekinah, 29–31; and
unborn, 32–33

Jacob, 32
Jansenism, 154
Jennings, Elizabeth, 168
Jeremiah, 32, 62
Jerome, St, 45
Jerusalem, 24
Jesus. *See* Son, the
John, St (evangelist), 77,
    106–7
John the Baptist, St, 84,
    93, 108, 131, 135; and
    Eucharist, 122; and
    Jesus, 32n, 91–92, 149;
    and Visitation, x, 24–
    28
John of the Cross, St, 169
John of Cyzicus, 9
John Damascene, St, 5, 8,
    56–57, 58, 70
John of Ford, 65–67
John Paul II, Pope, 27n, 71,
    125; on Eucharist, 116;
    on Mary, 5, 49n, 105–6,
    128, 134, 149; *Mulieris
    dignitatem*, 105, 133–34;
    on womanhood, 105–6,
    116–17, 133–34
Joseph, St, 93, 94, 149; and
    David, 41–42; humility
    of, 38–42; and Mary, 37–
    42, 167, 169

La Tour, Georges de, 83
Laurentin, René, 27n, 40